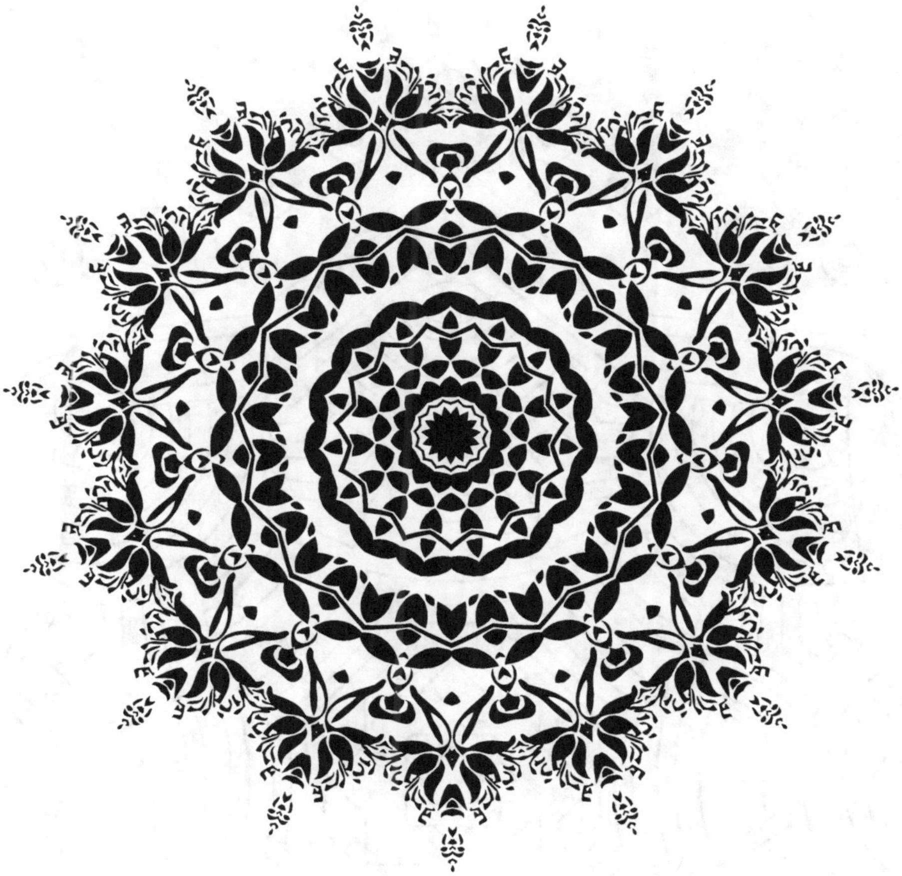

Mandala

Coloring Book

FOR KIDS

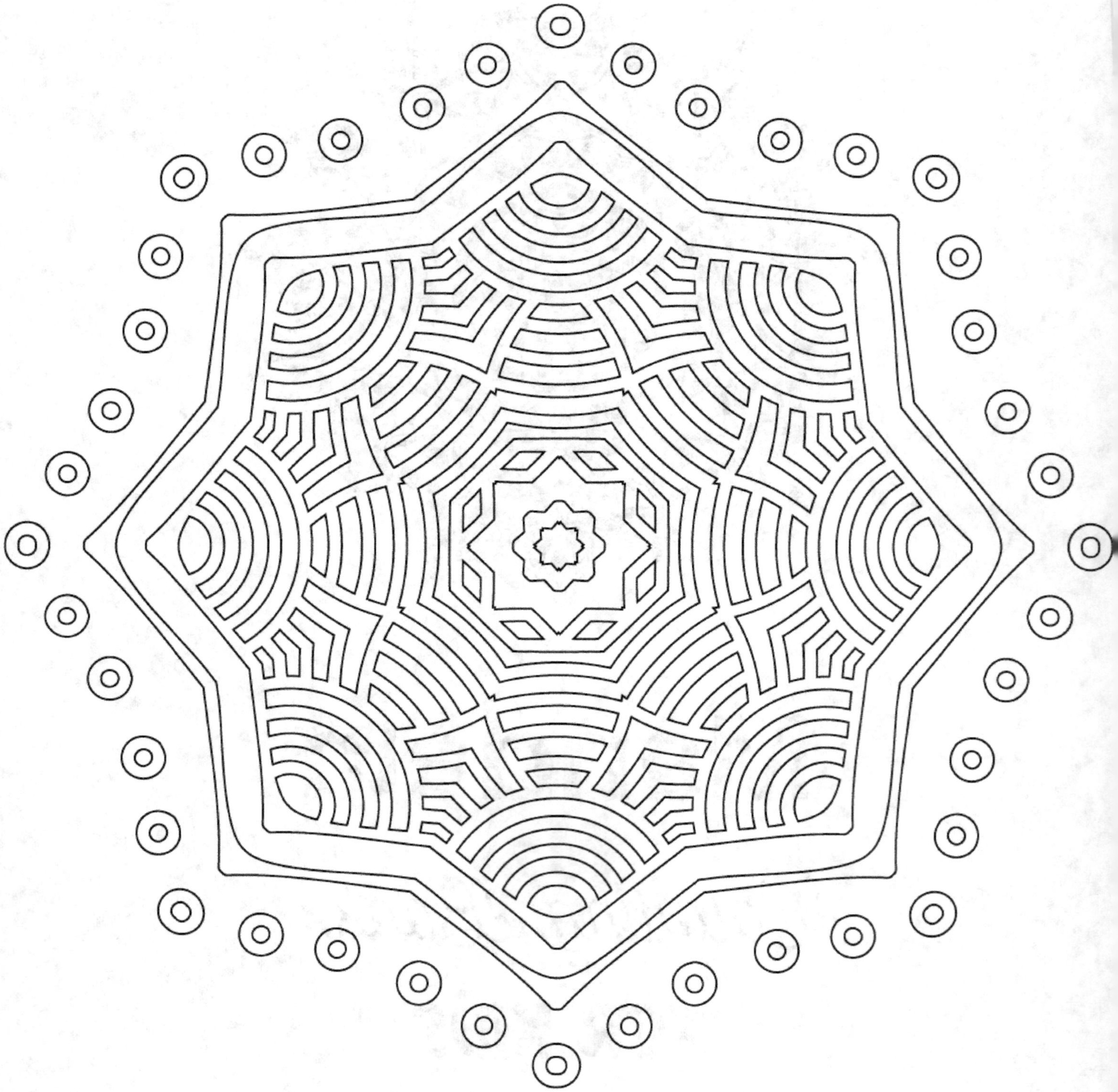

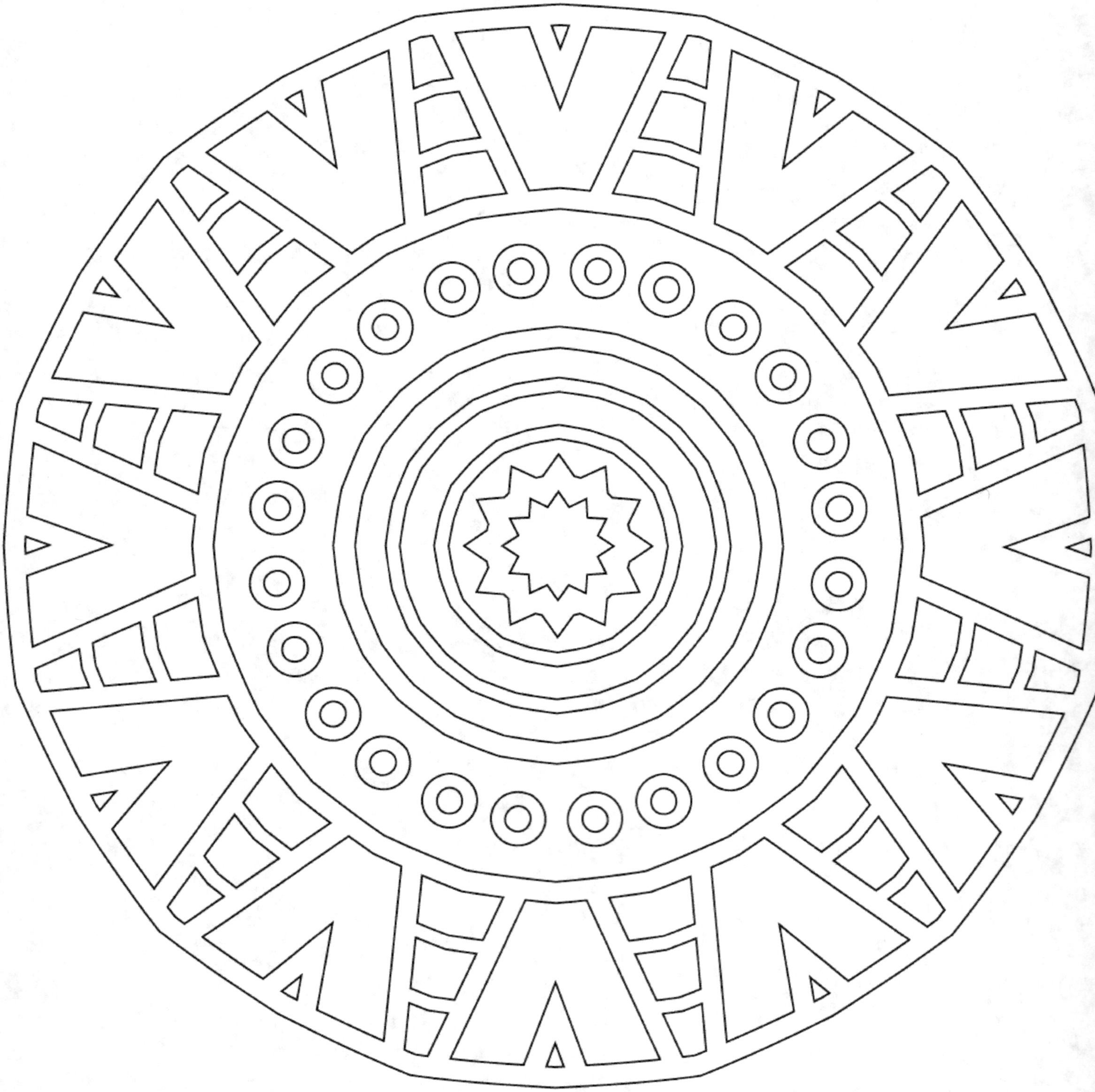

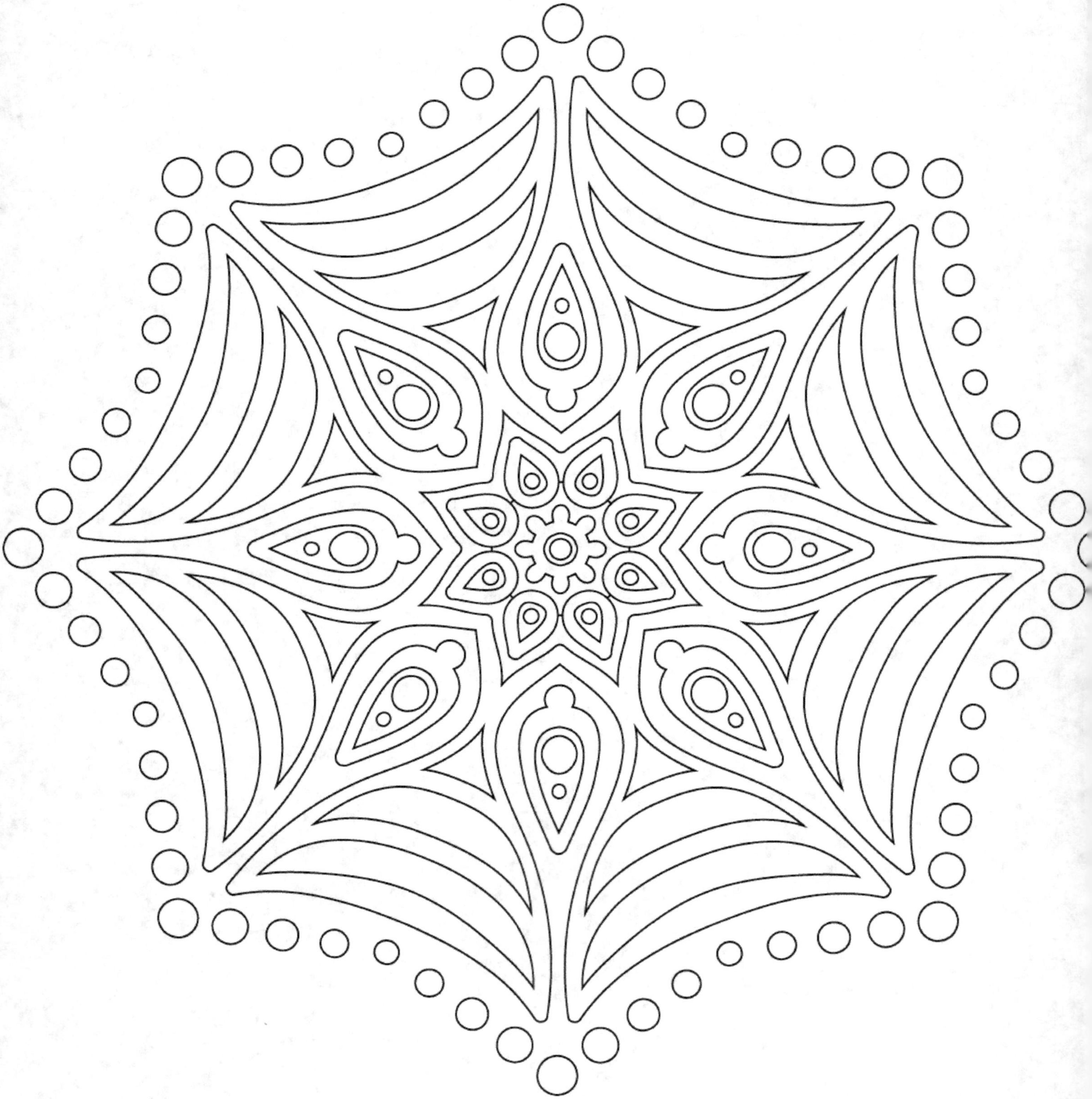

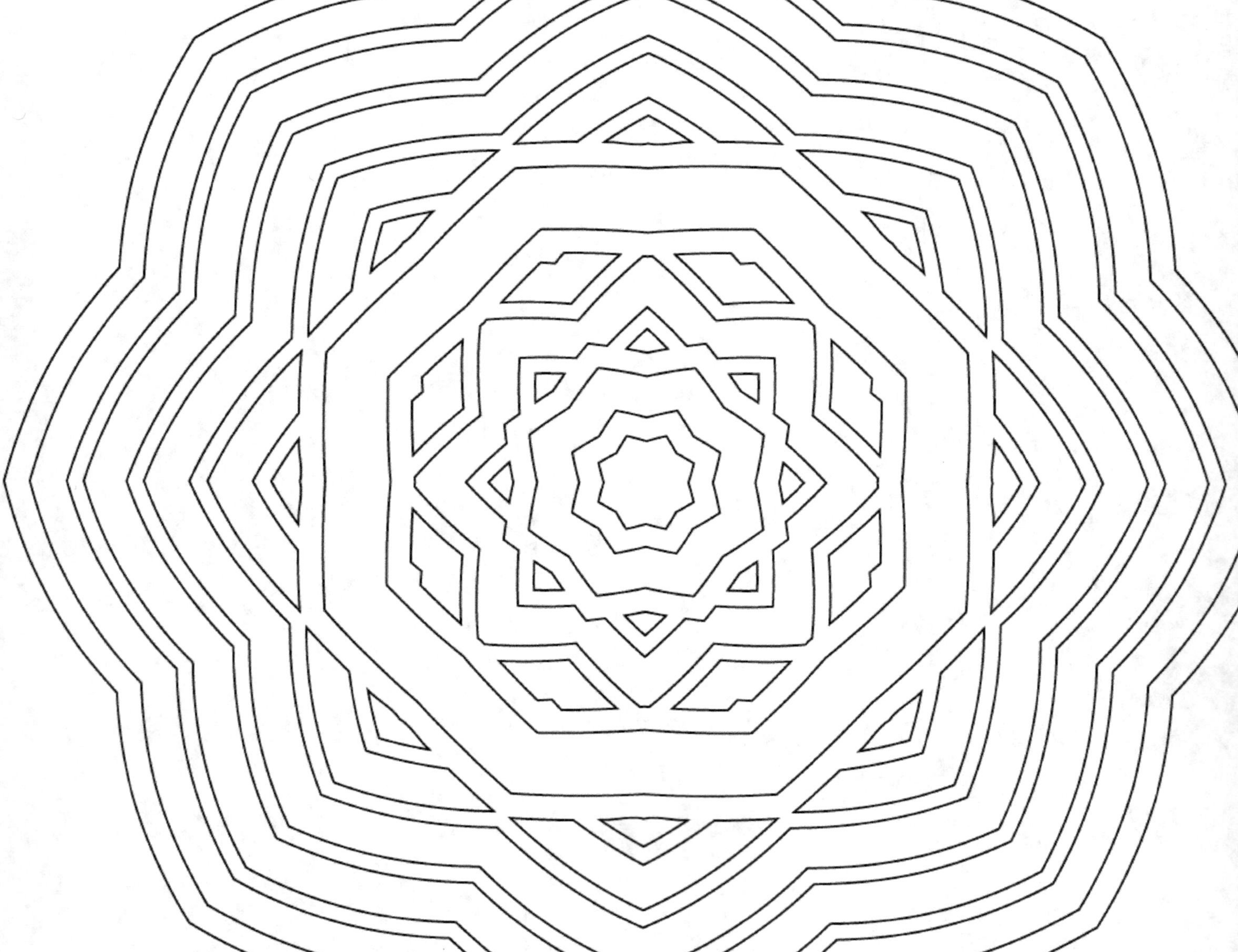

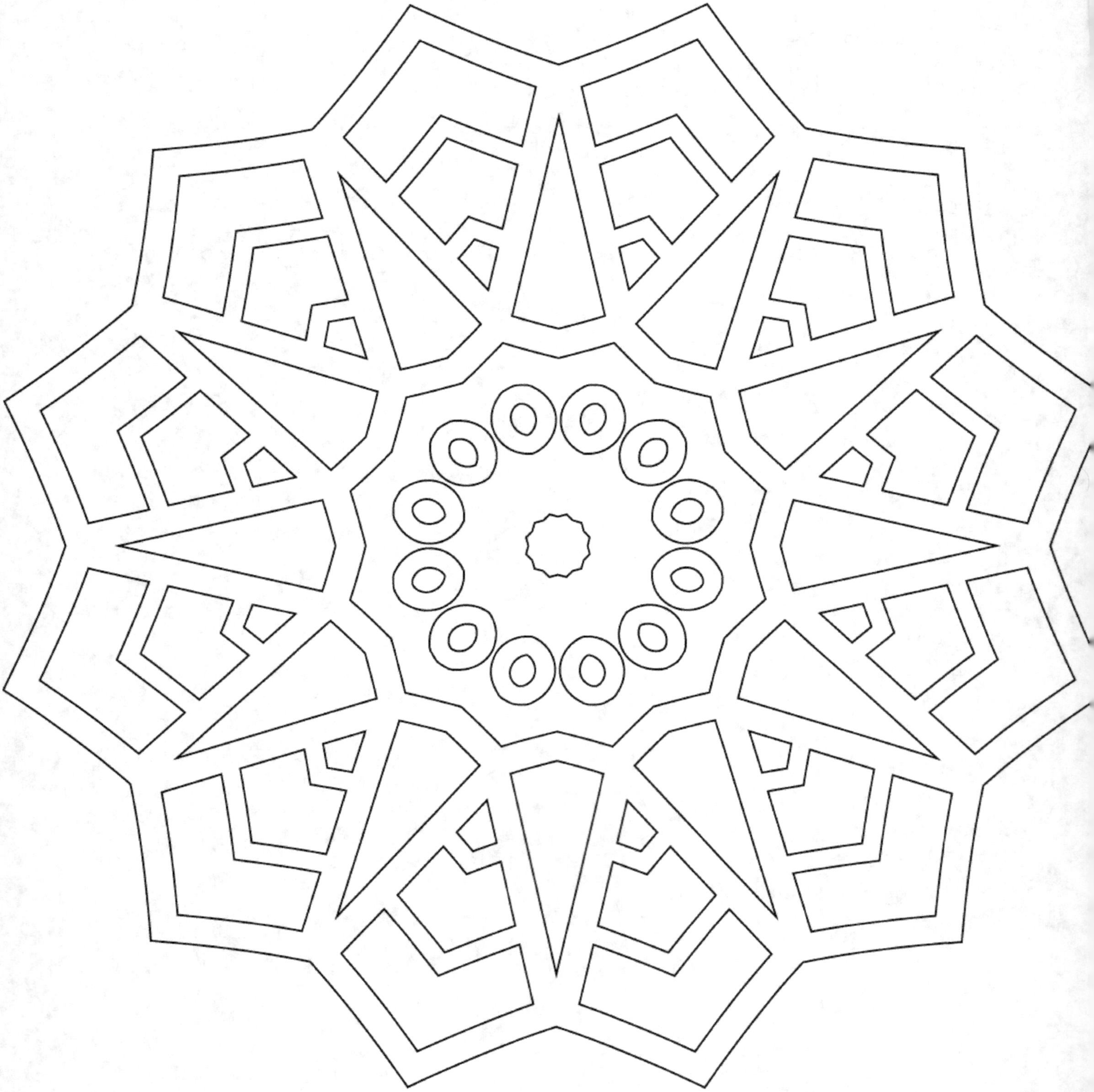

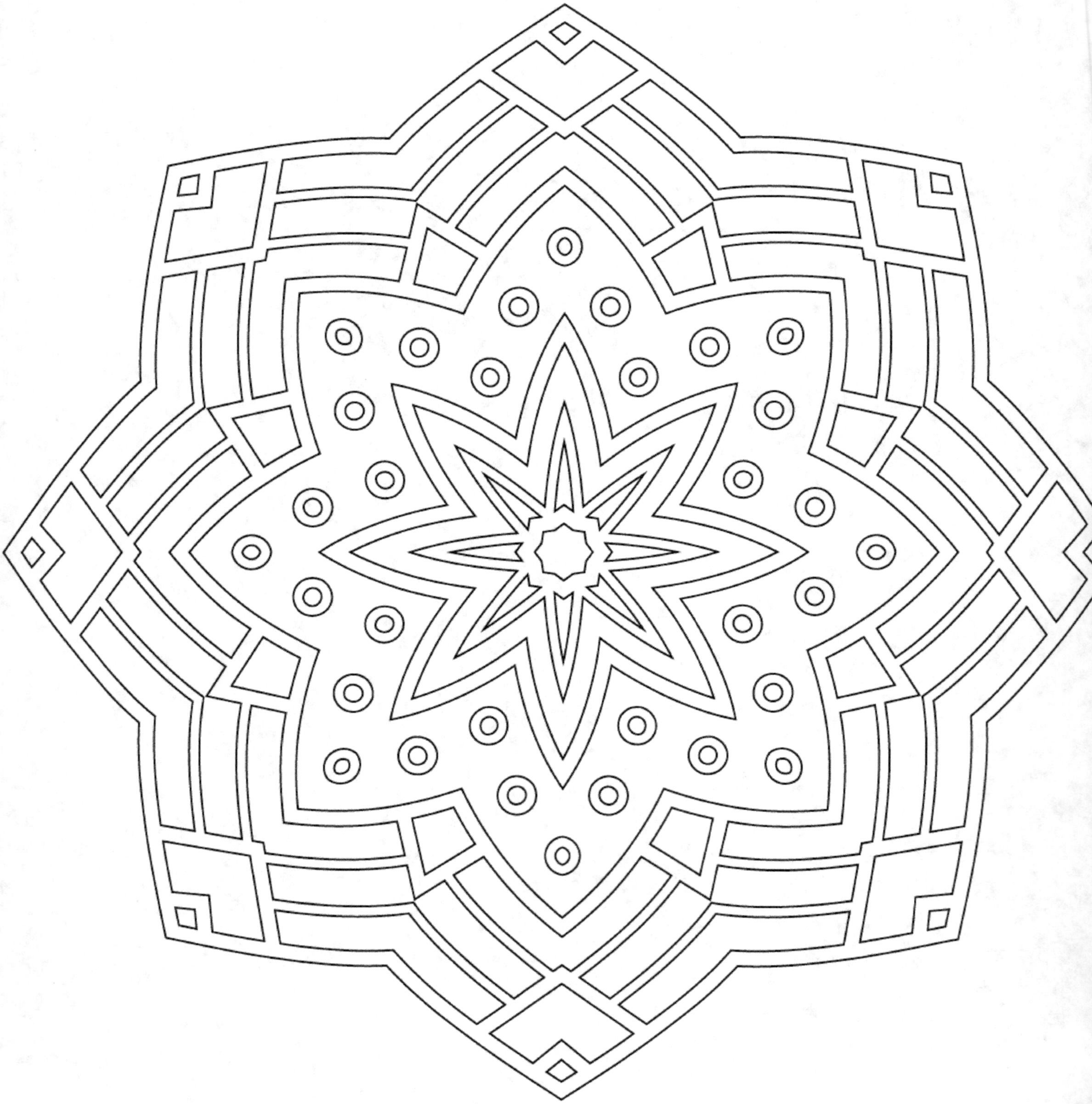

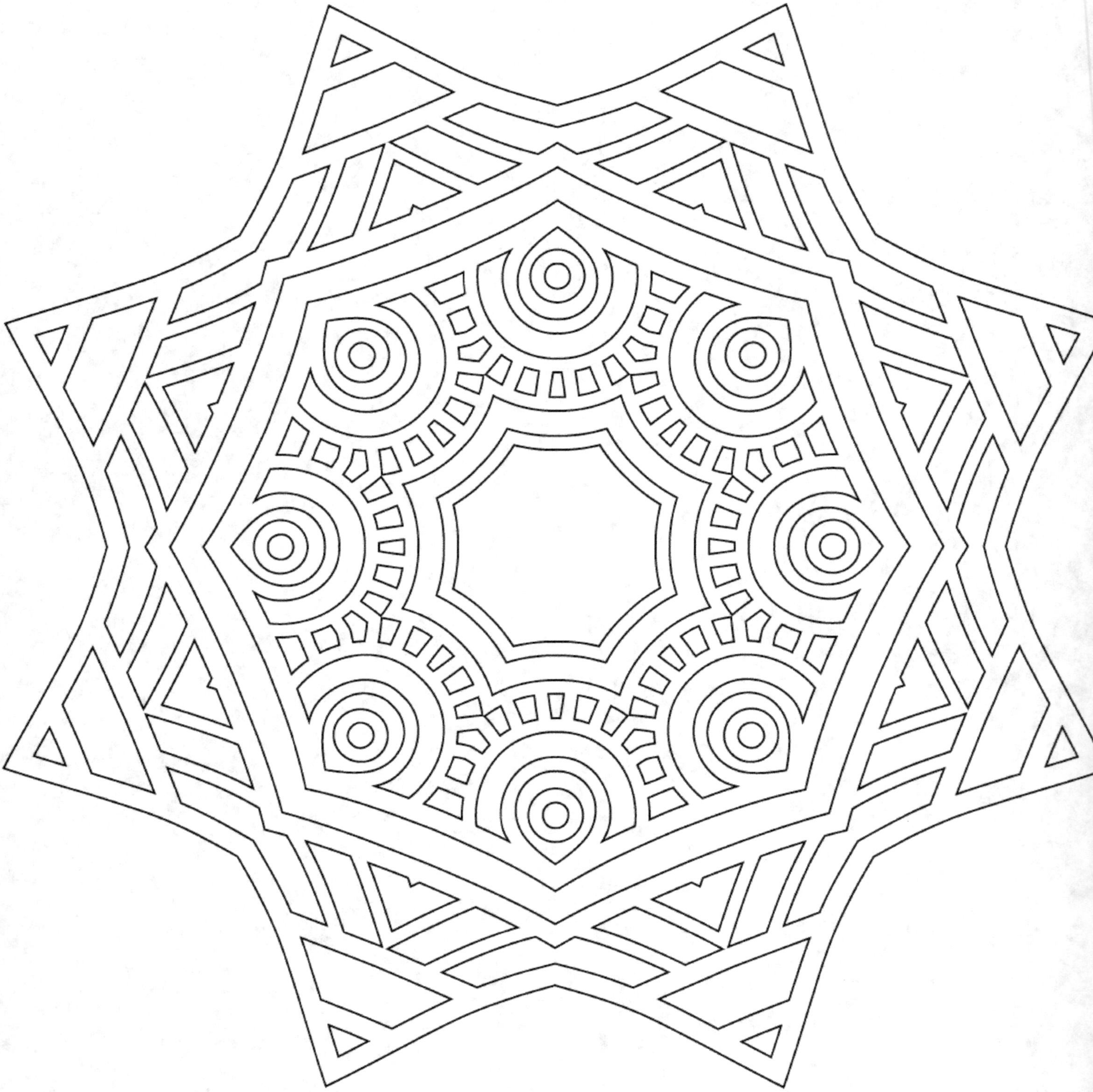

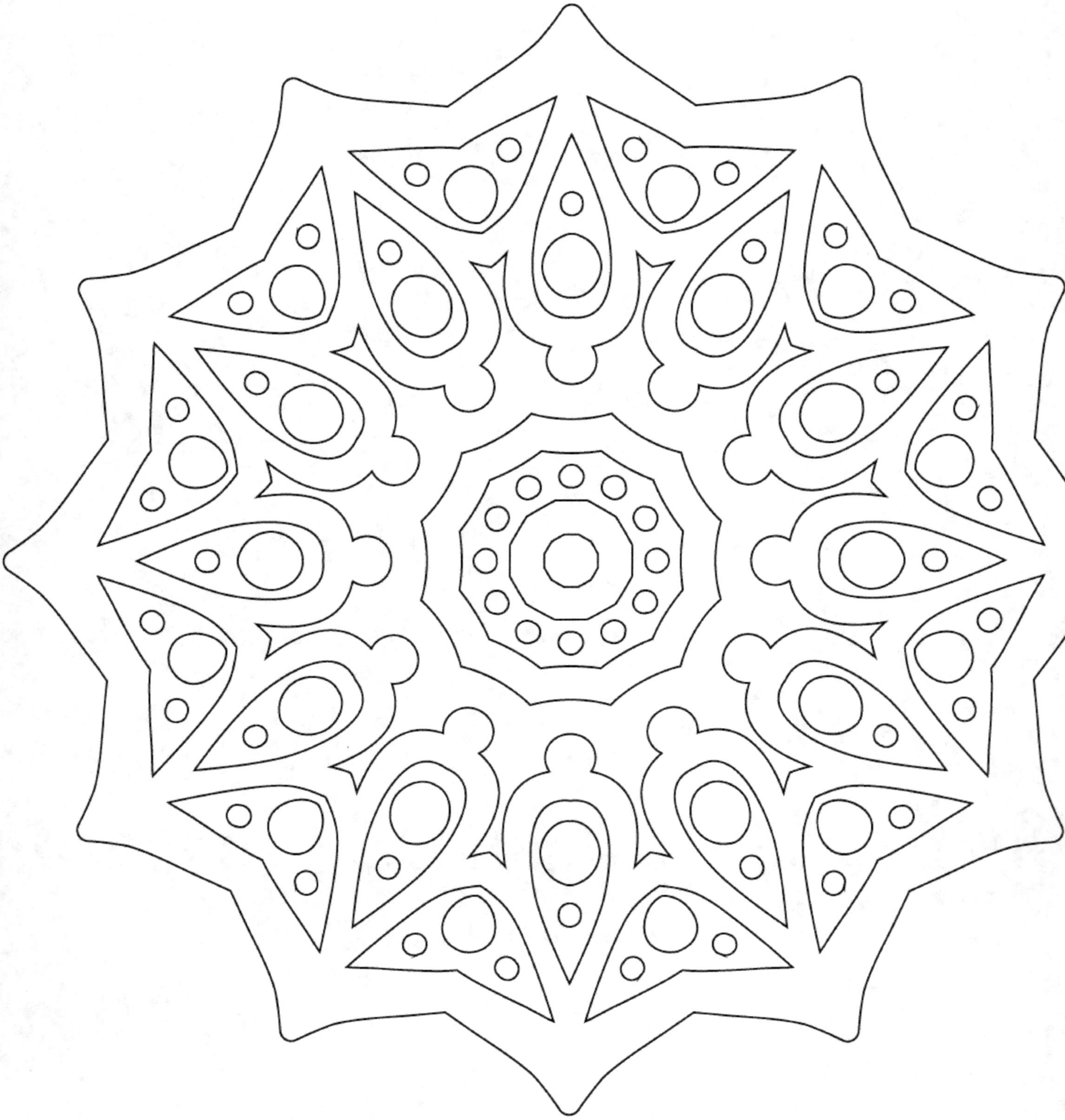

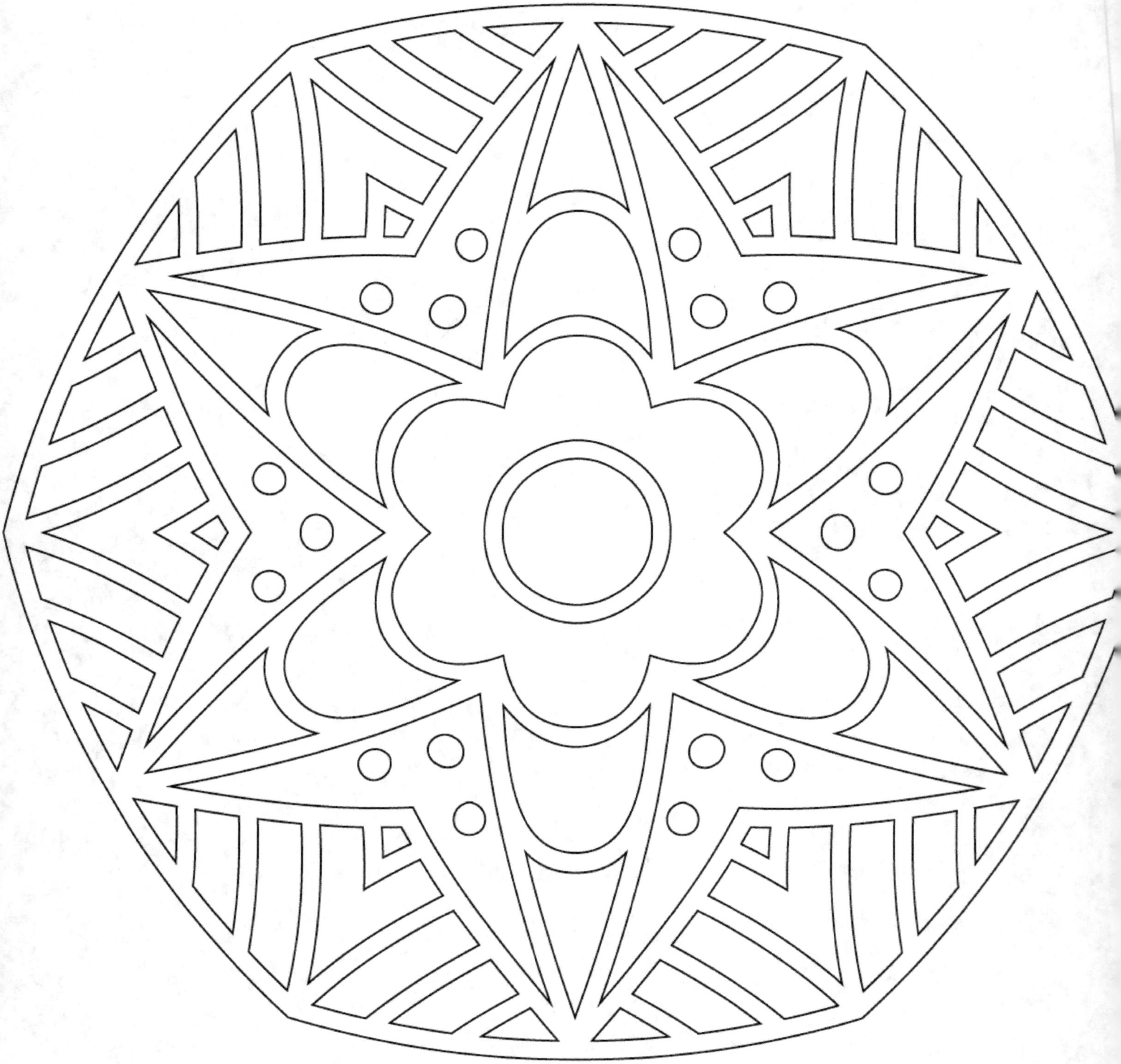

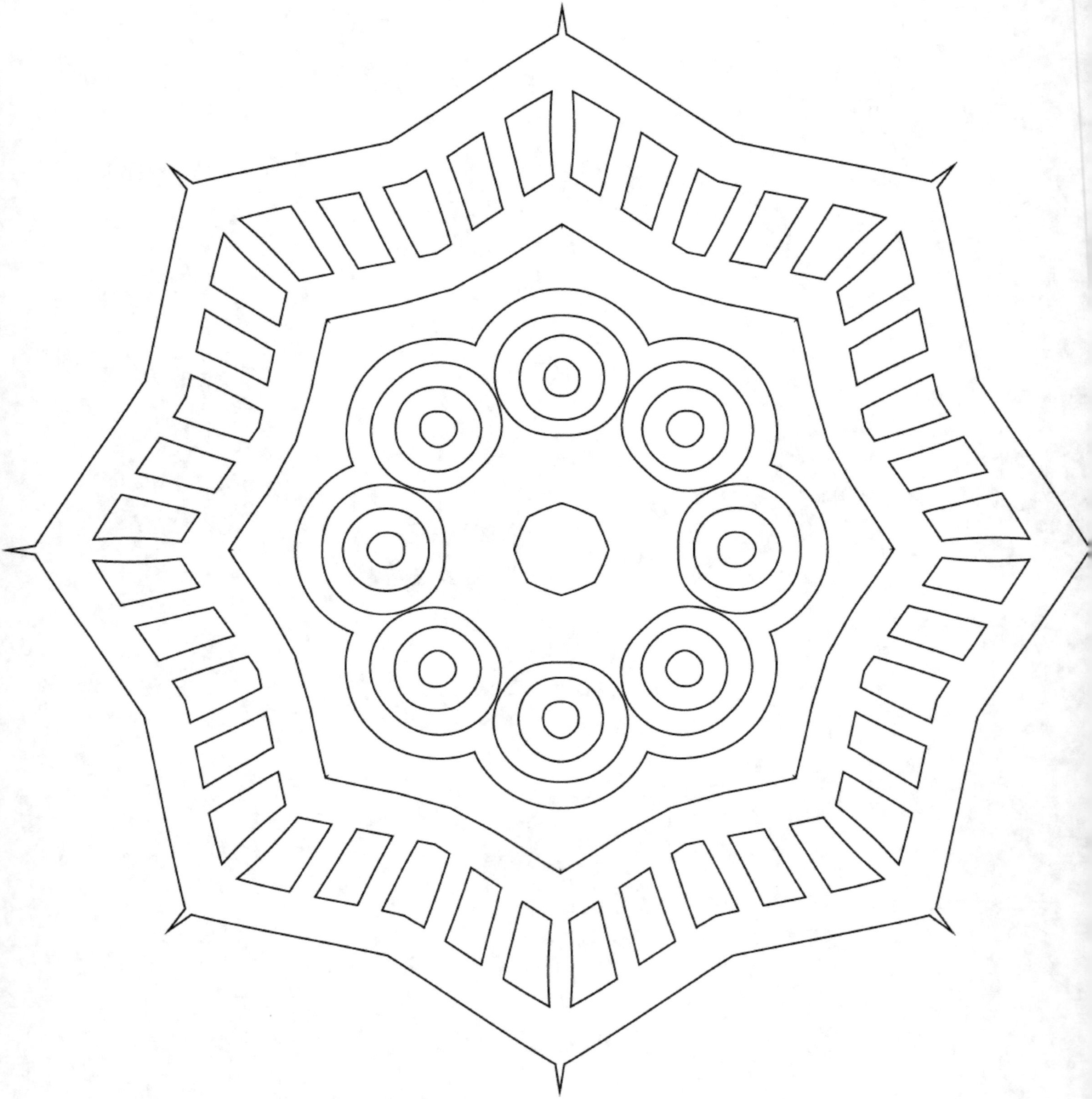

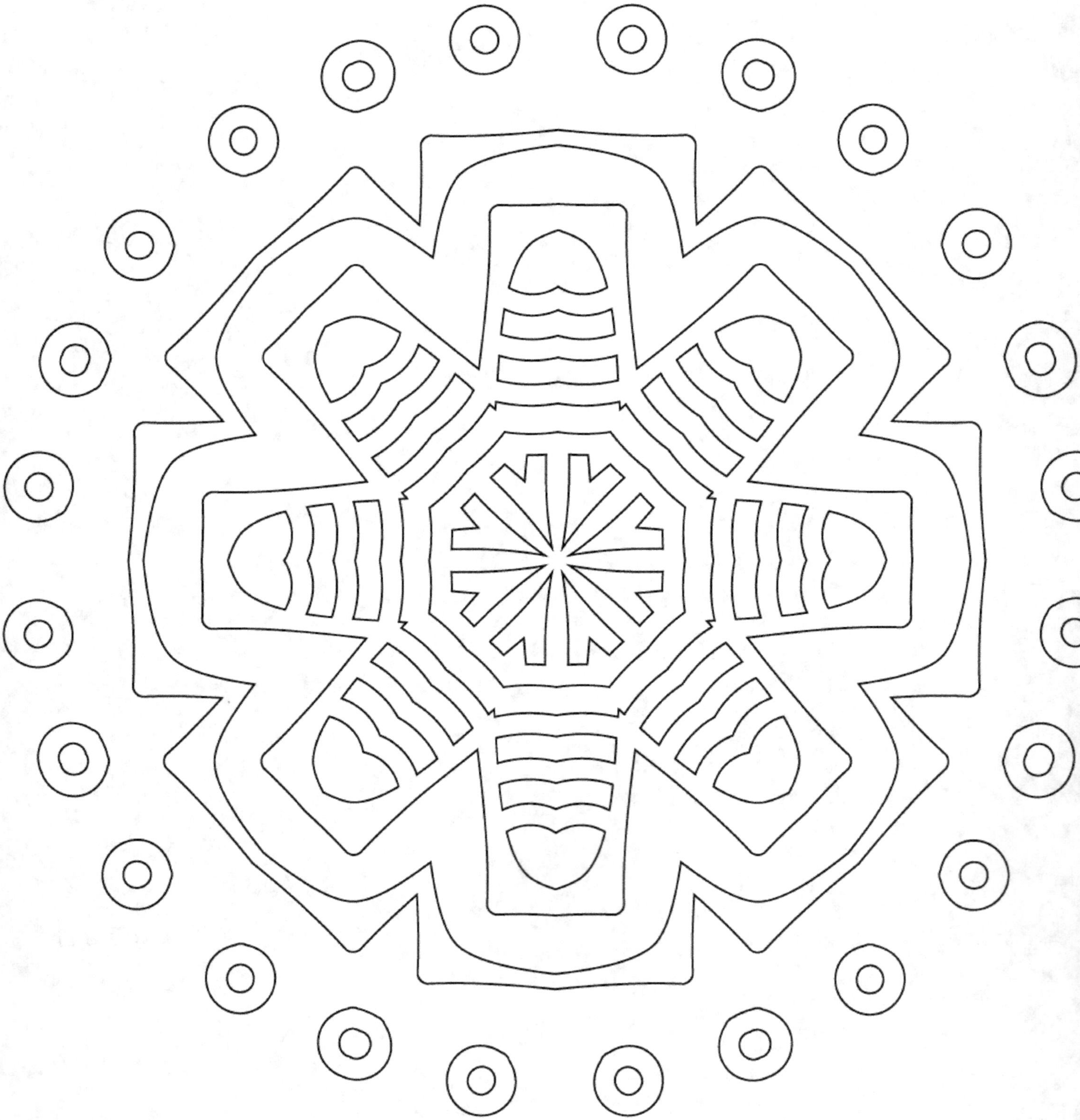

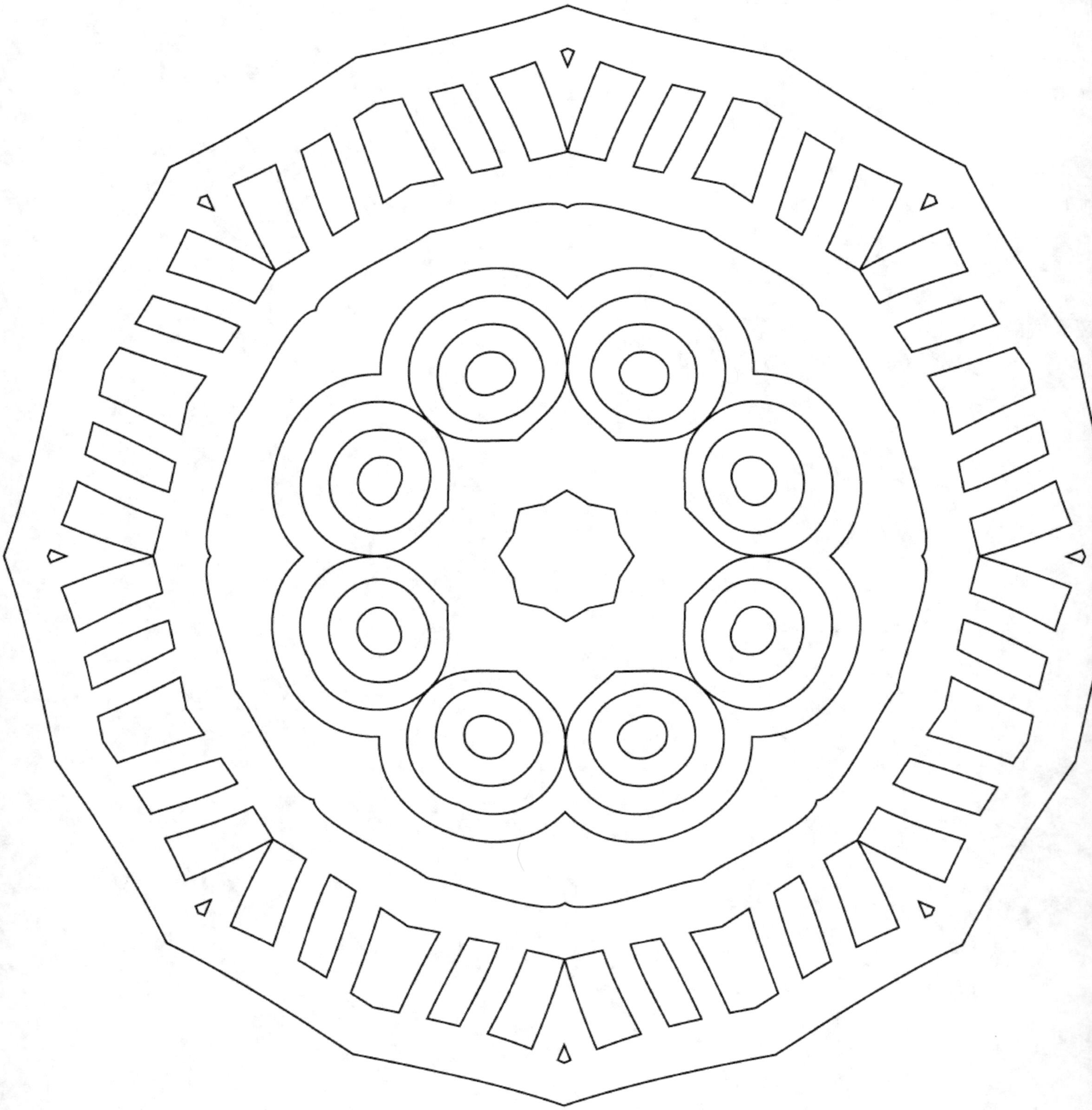

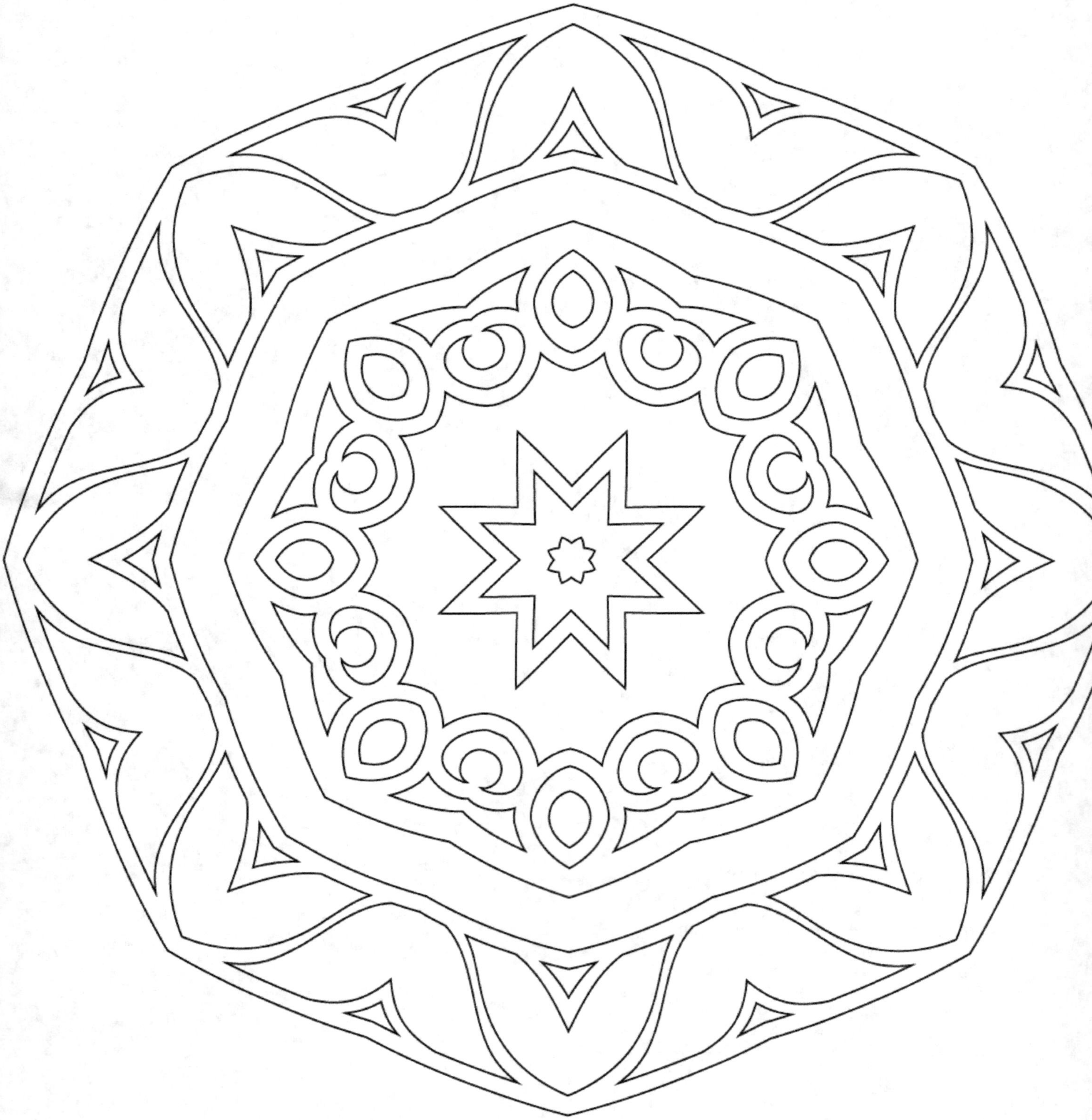

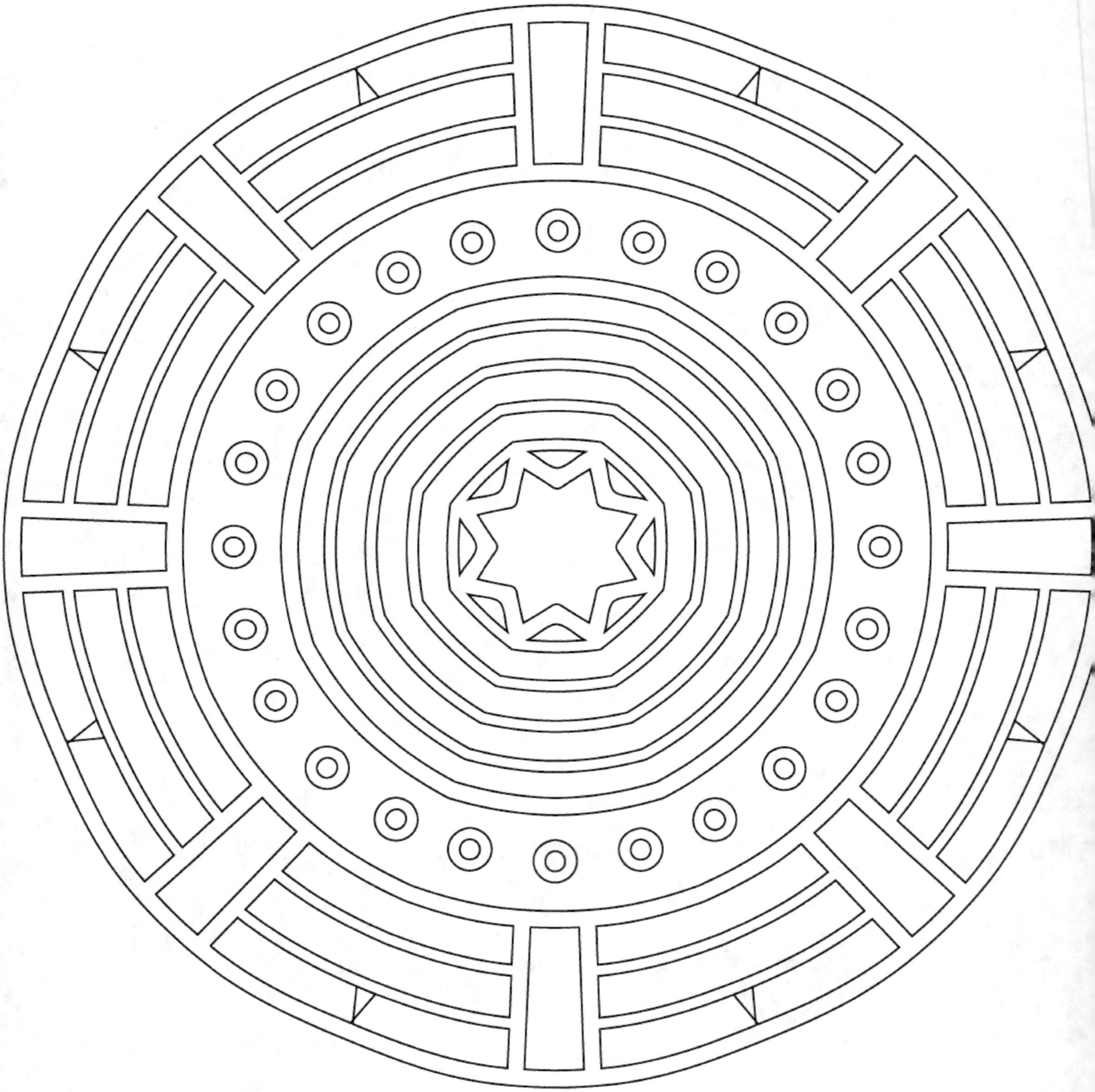

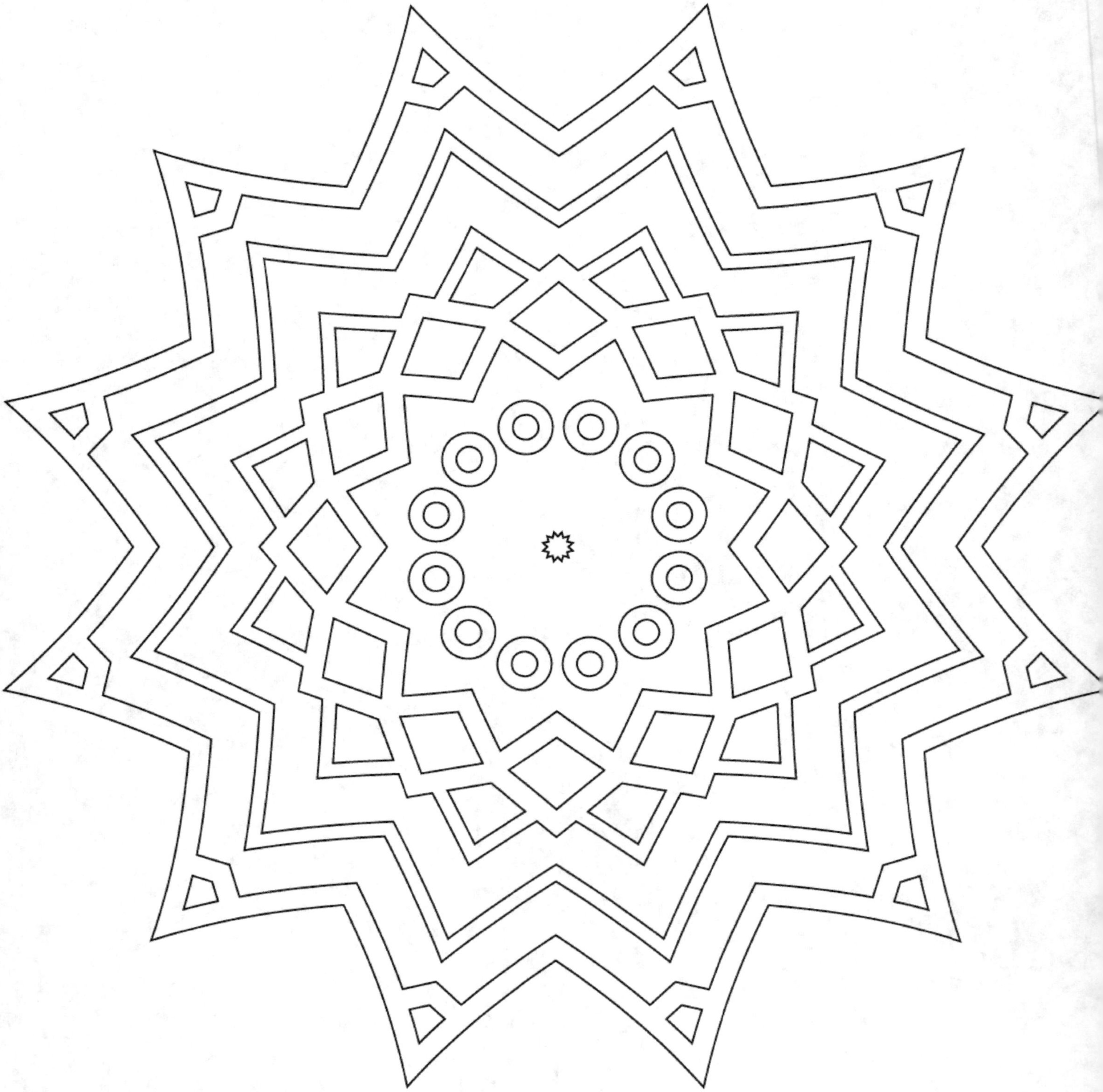

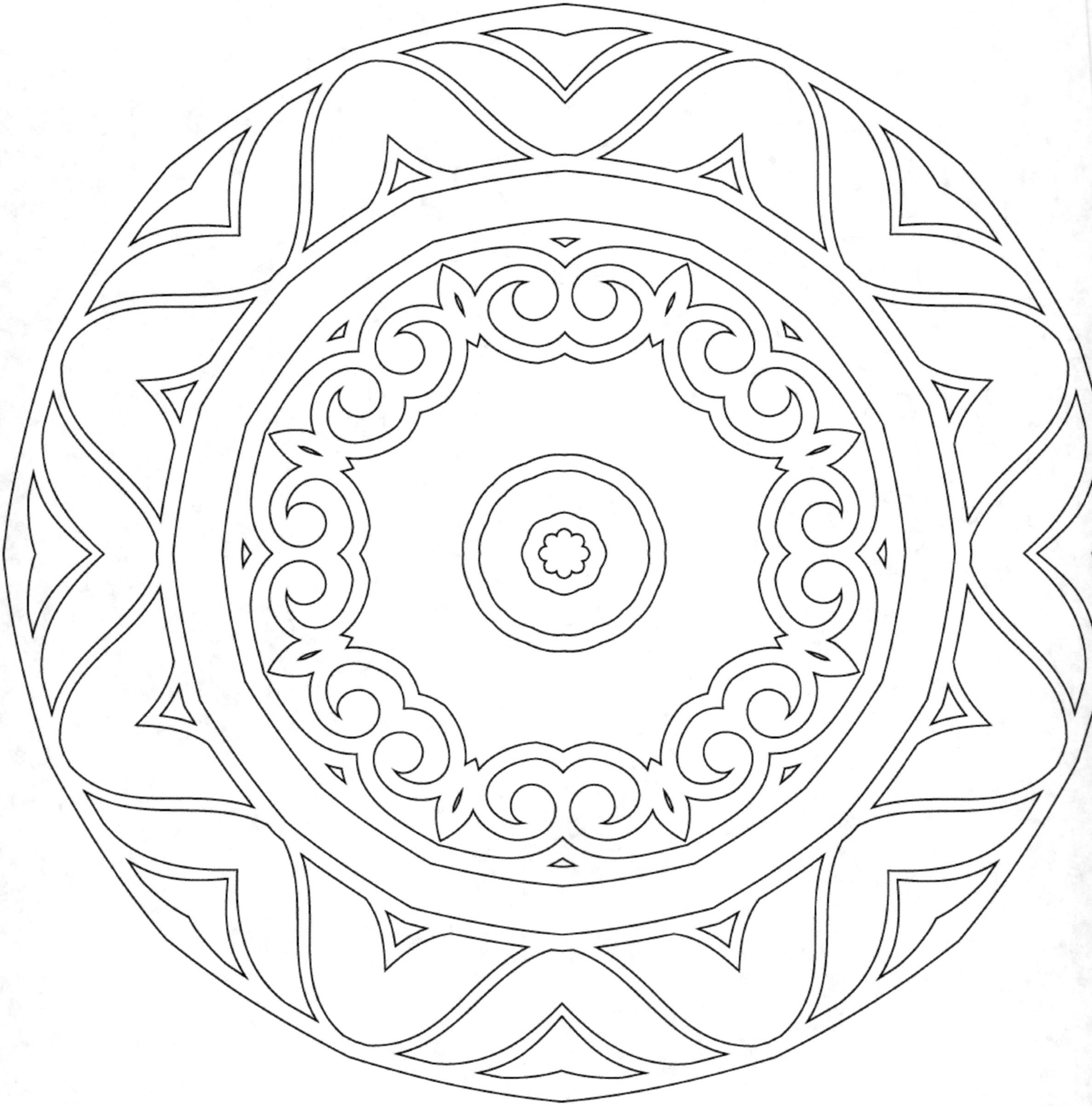

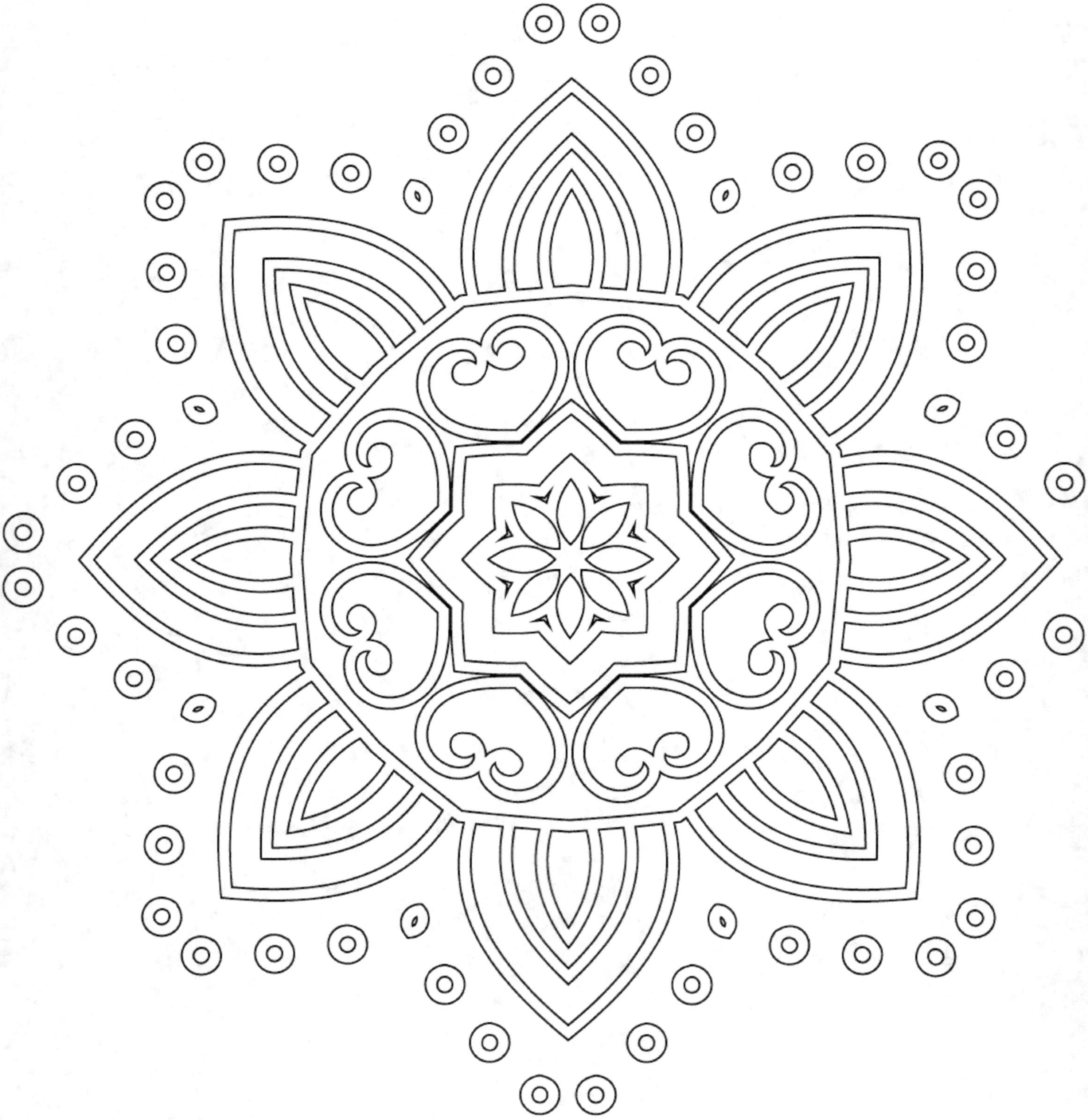

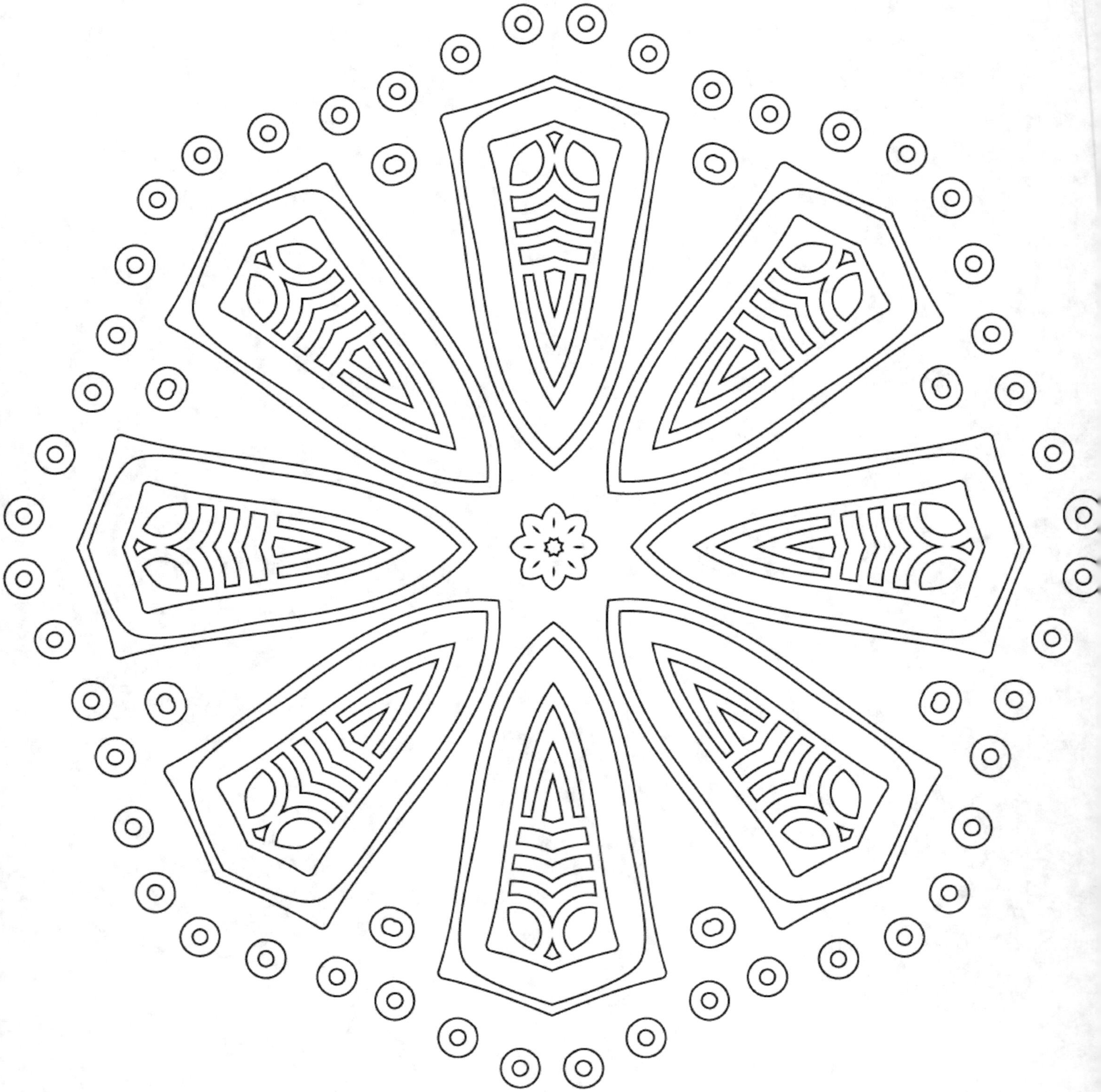

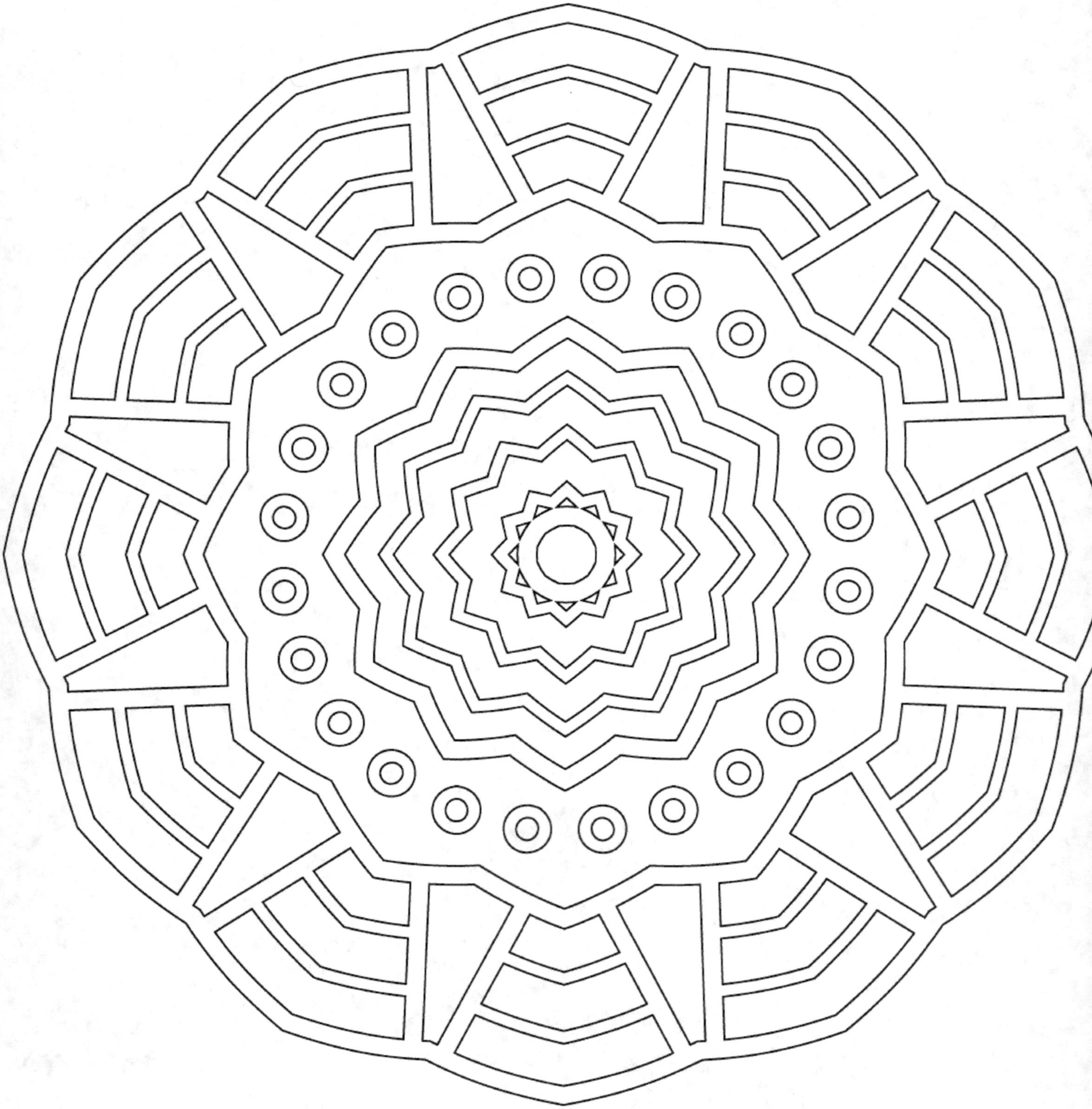

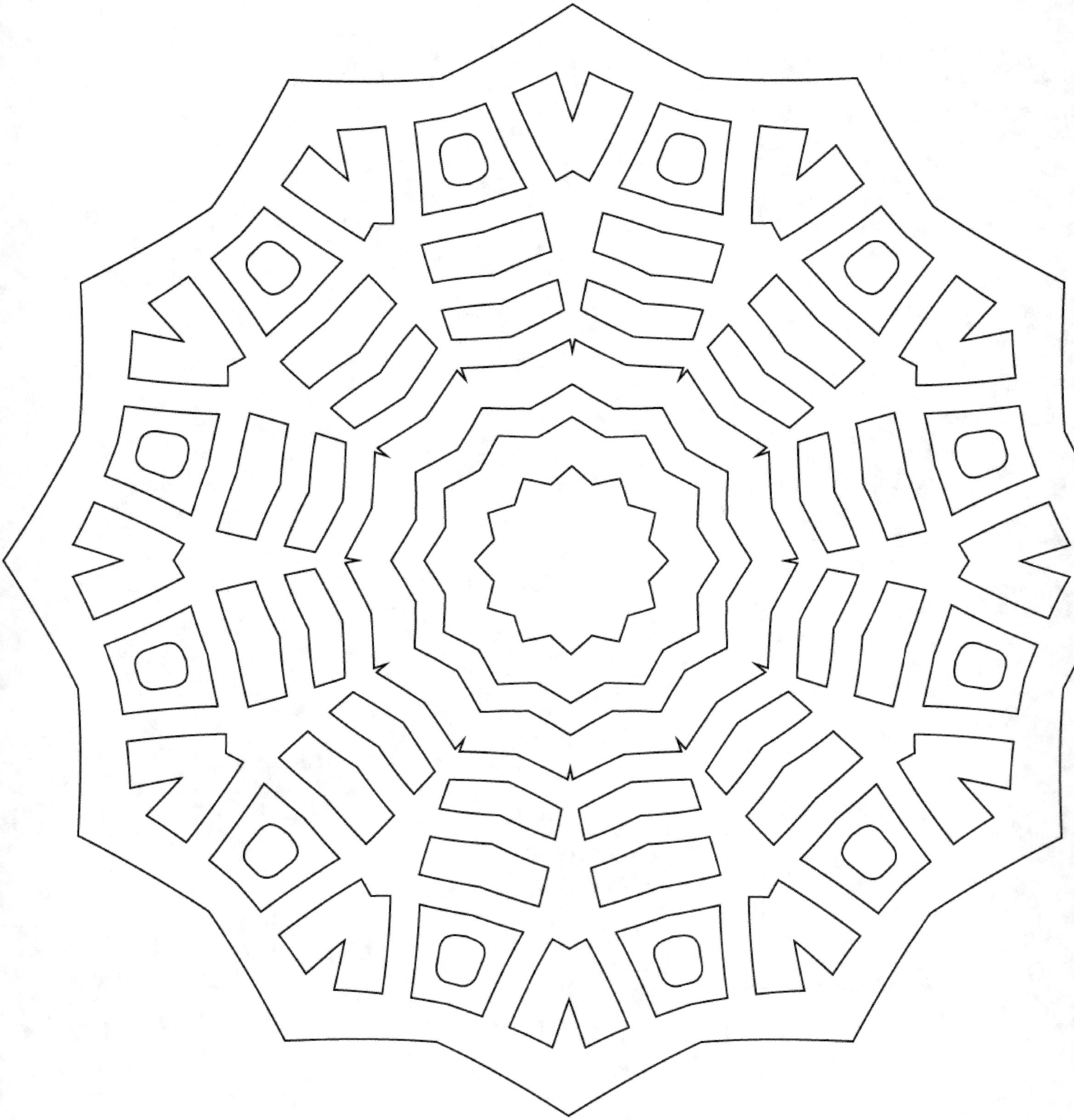

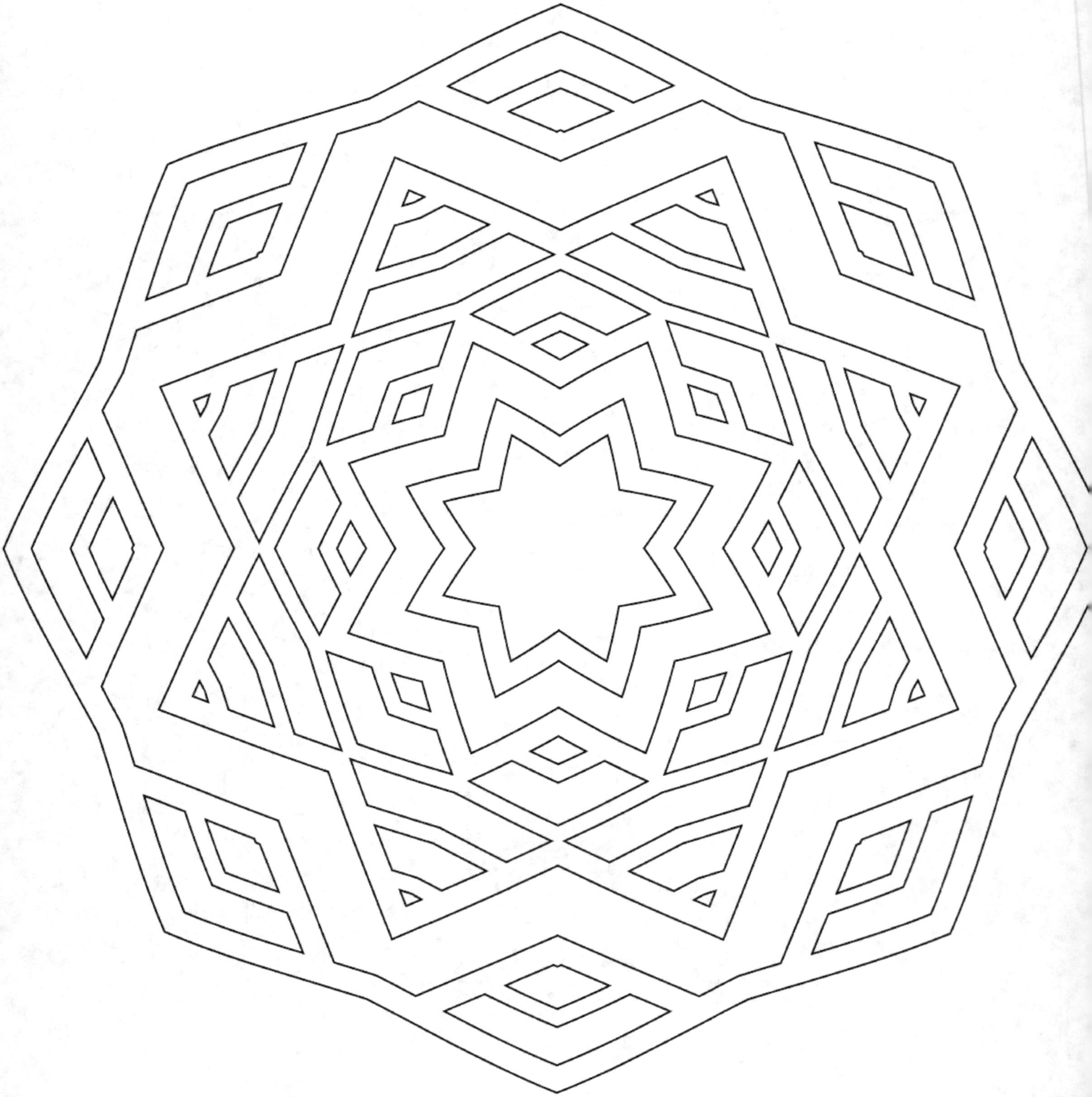

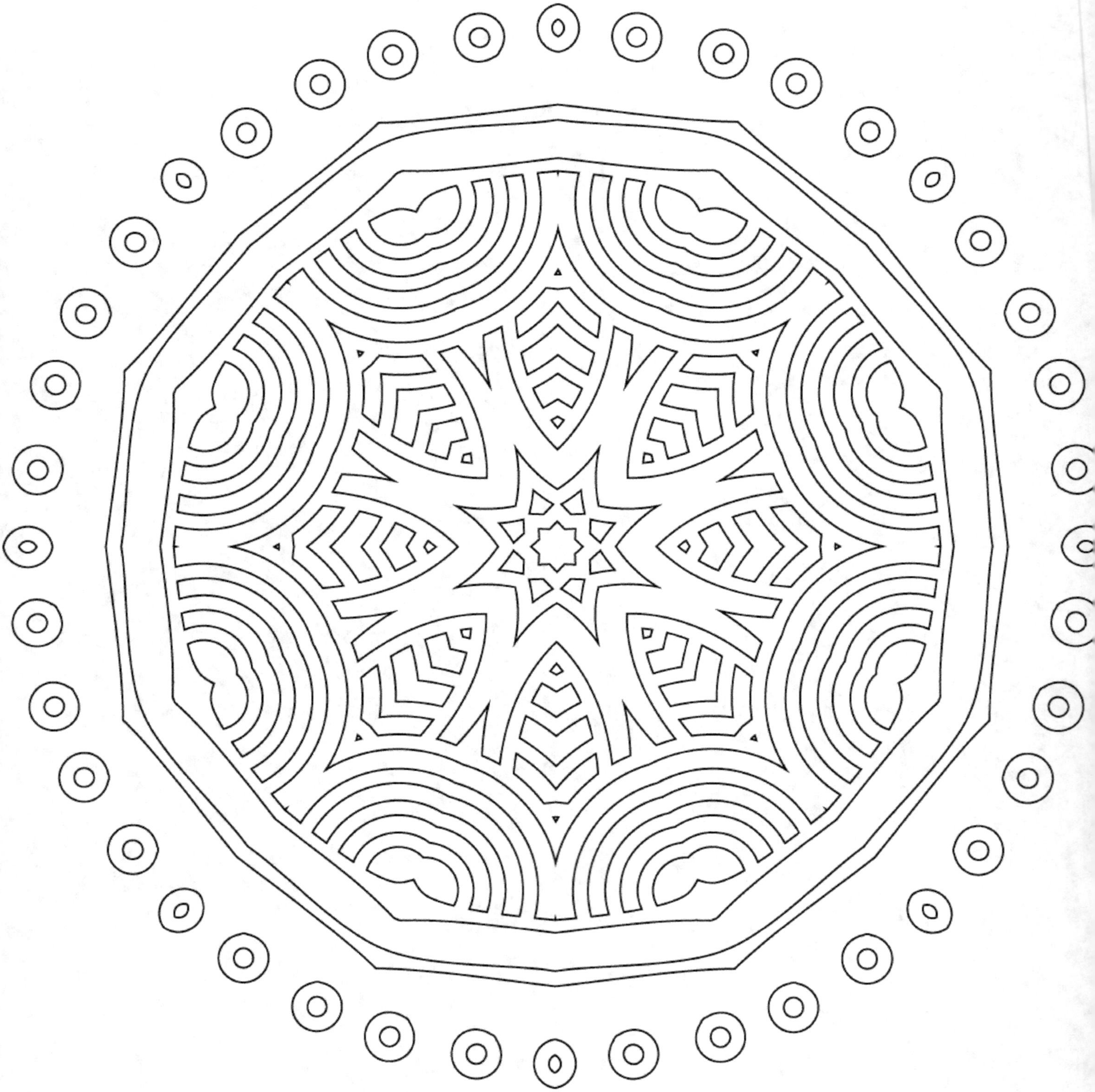

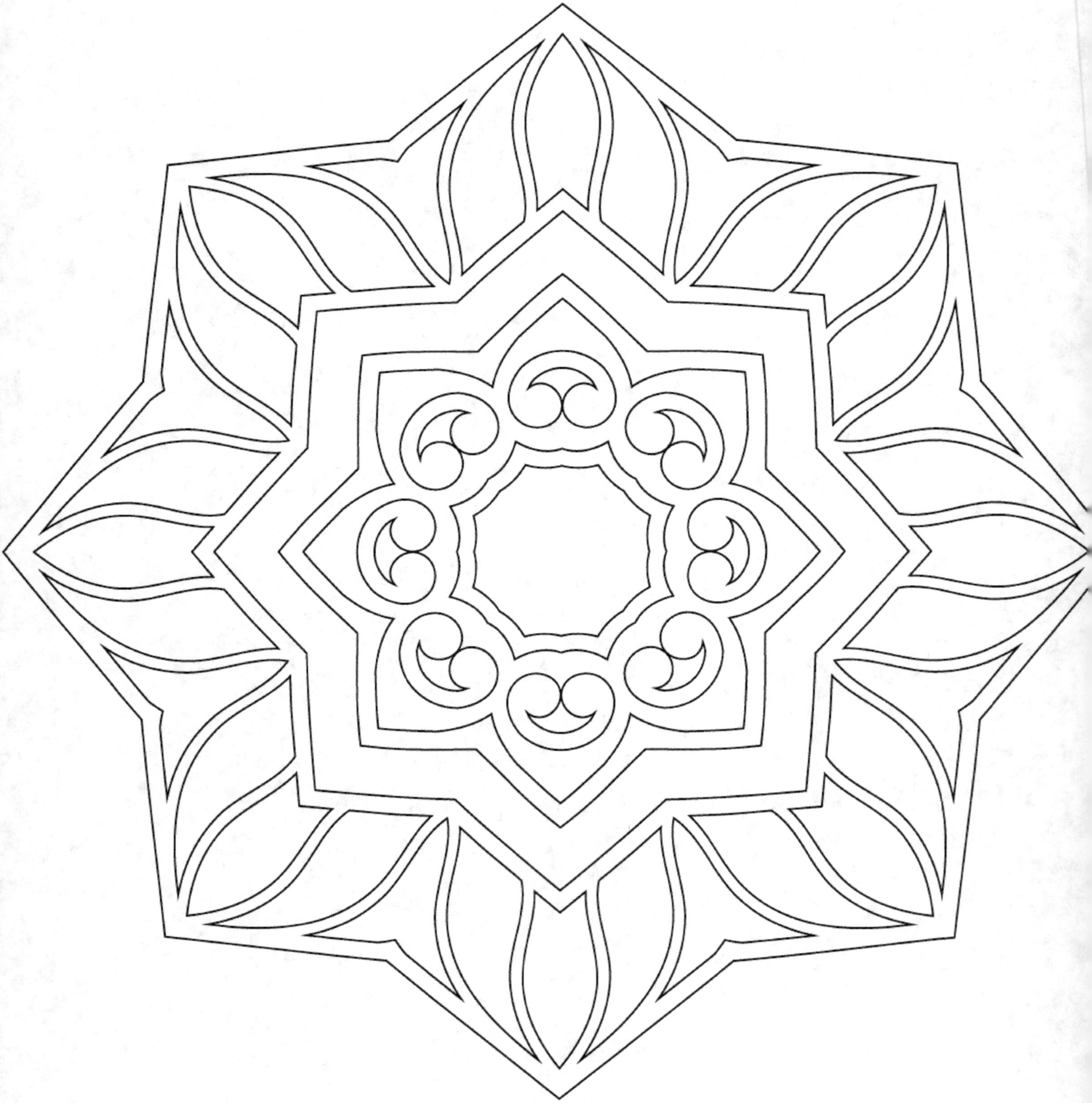

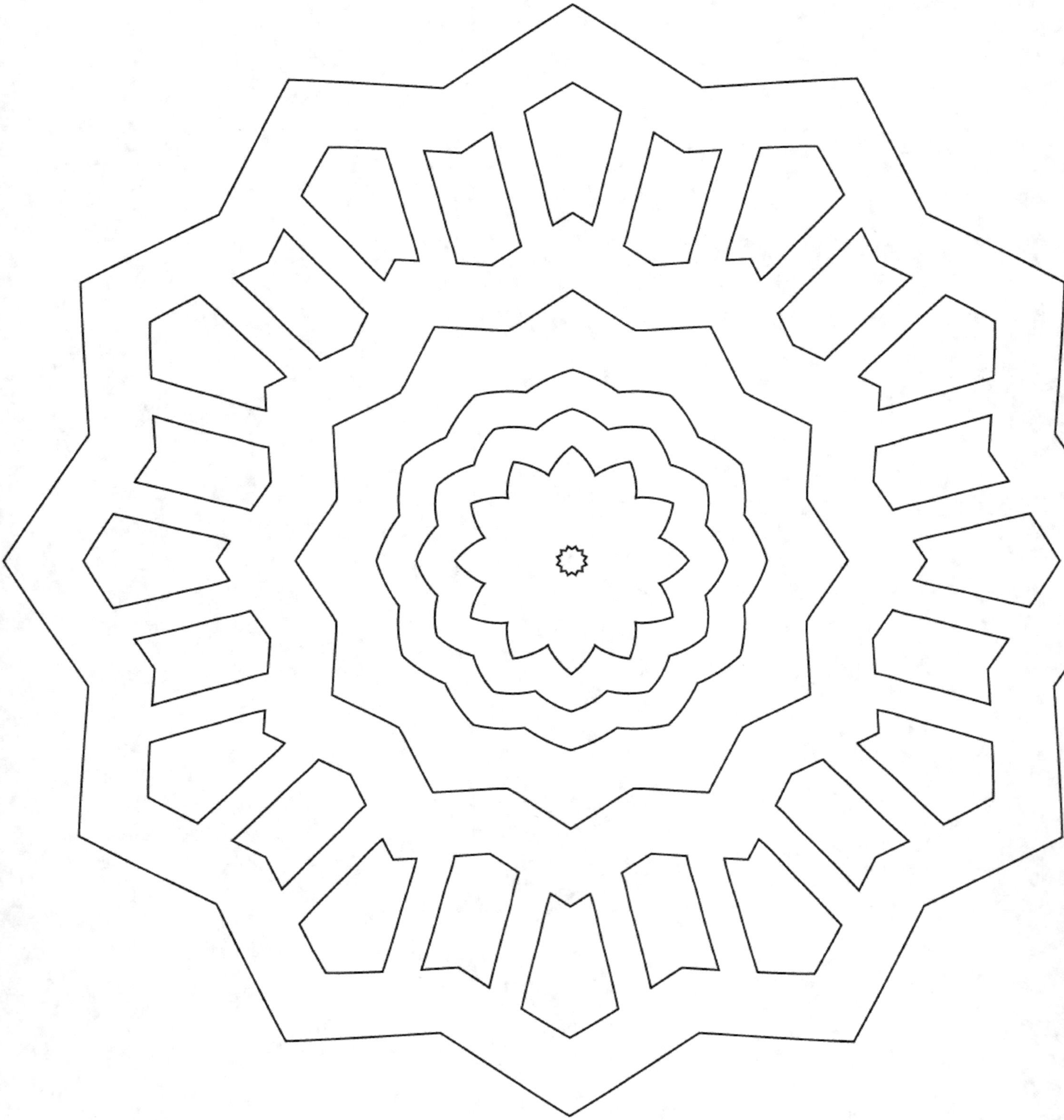

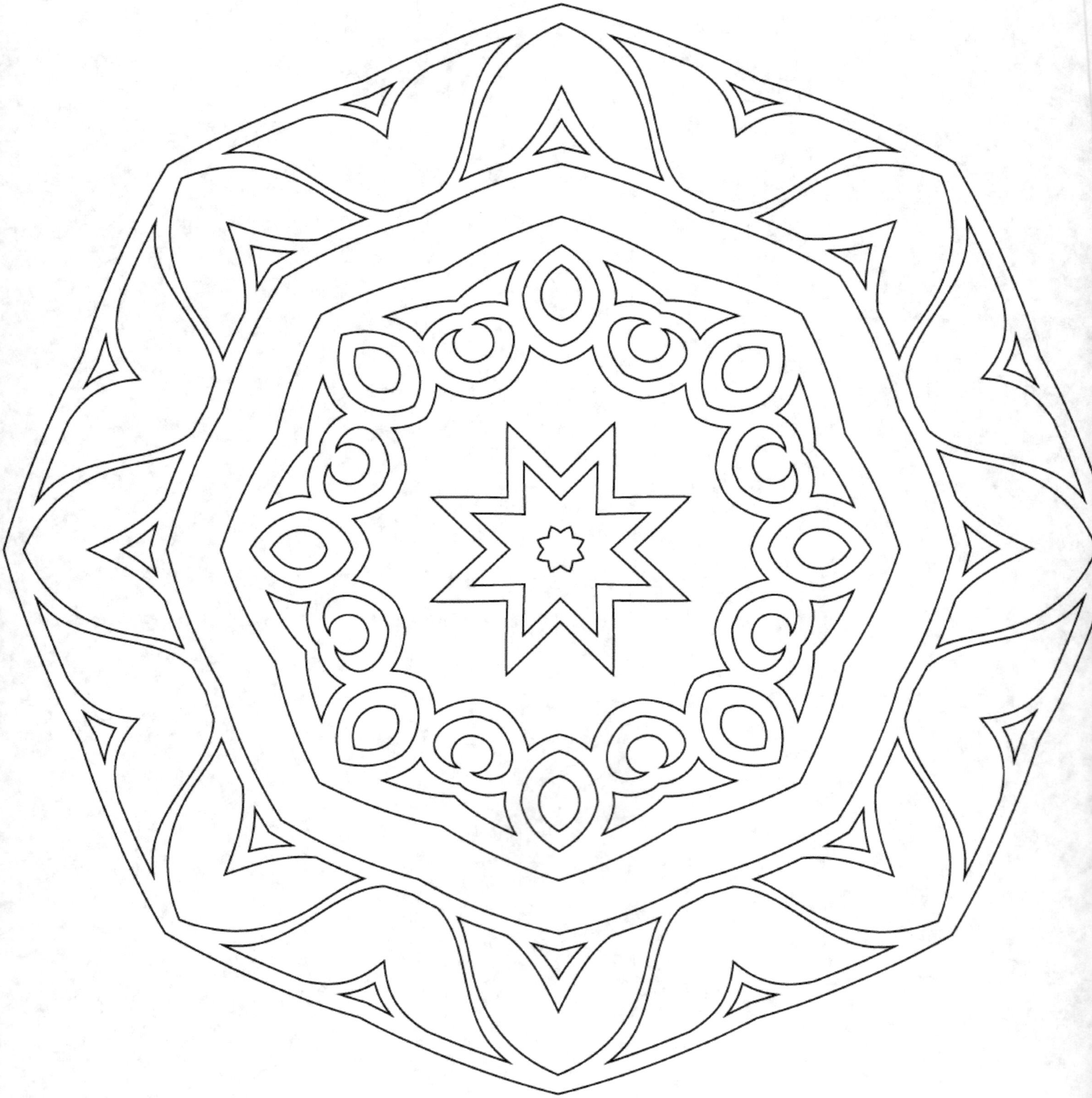

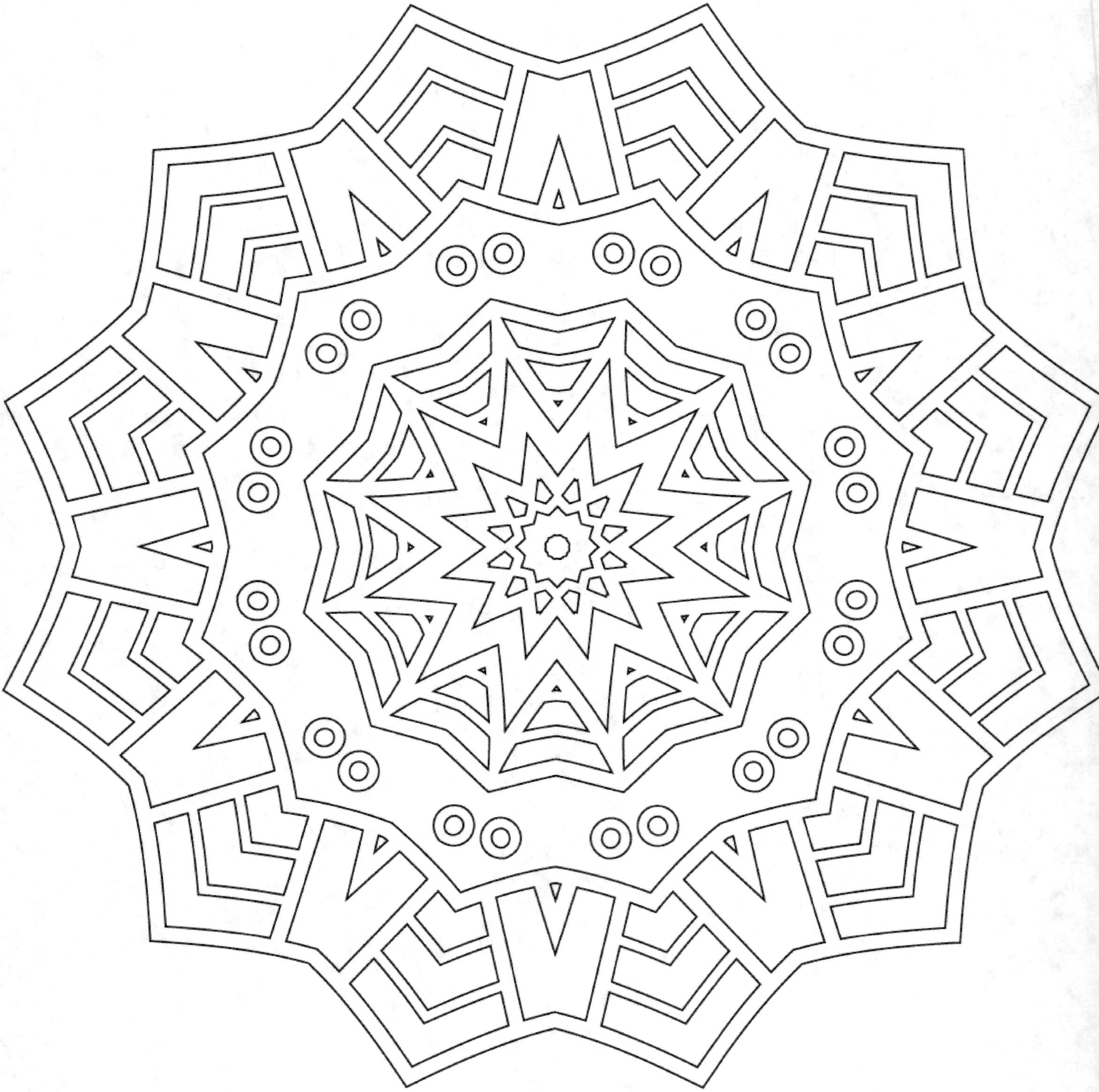

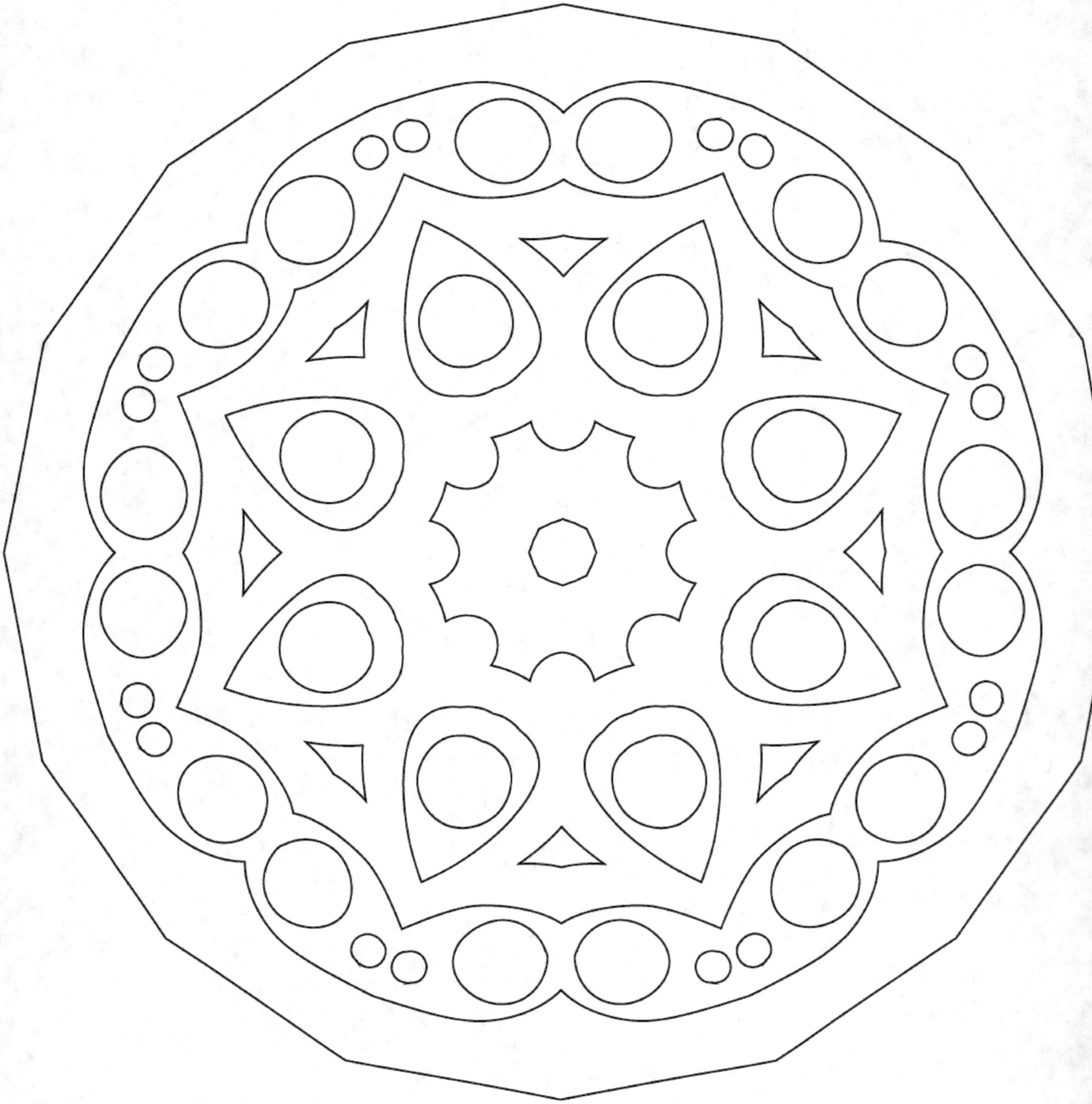

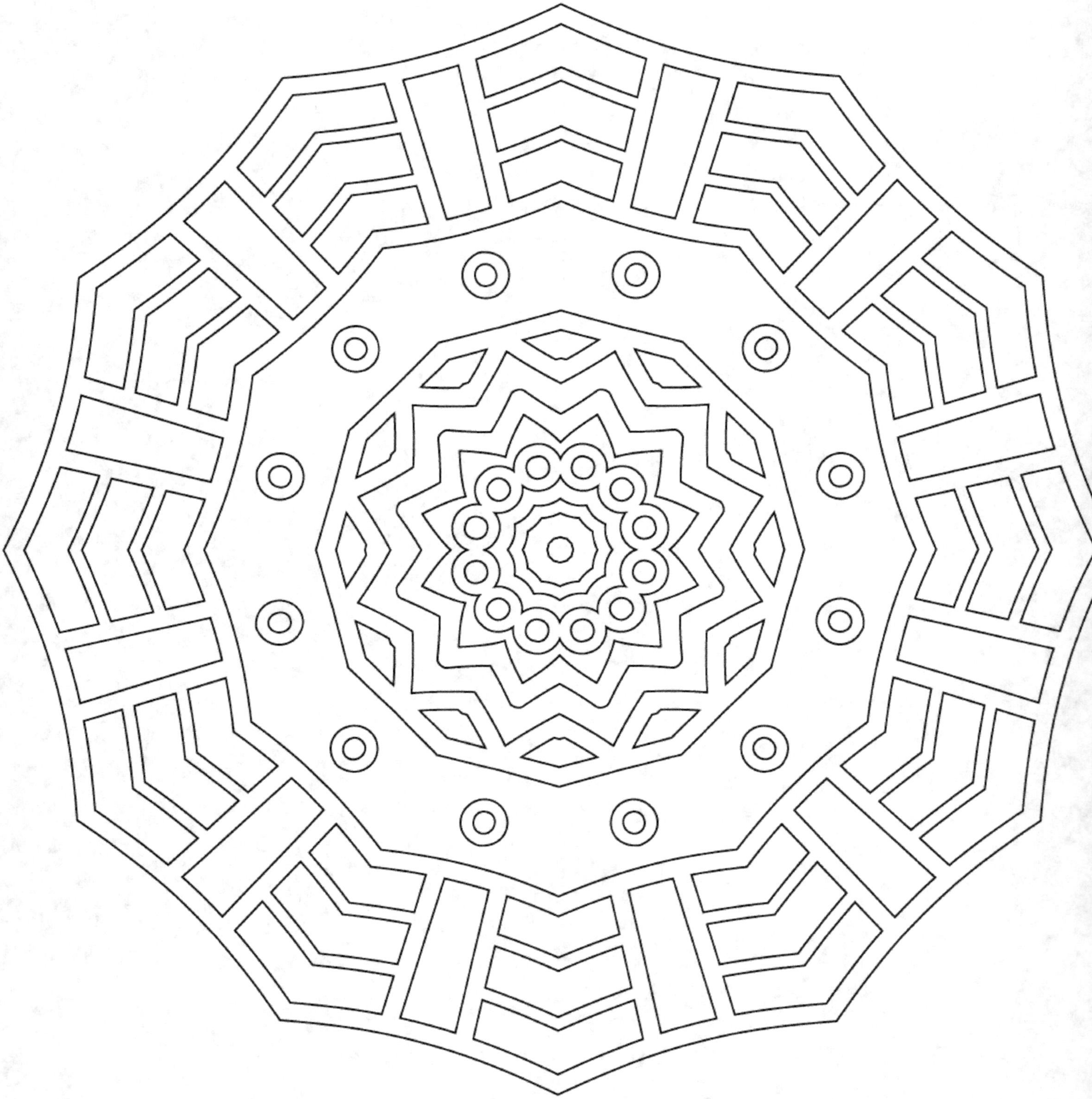

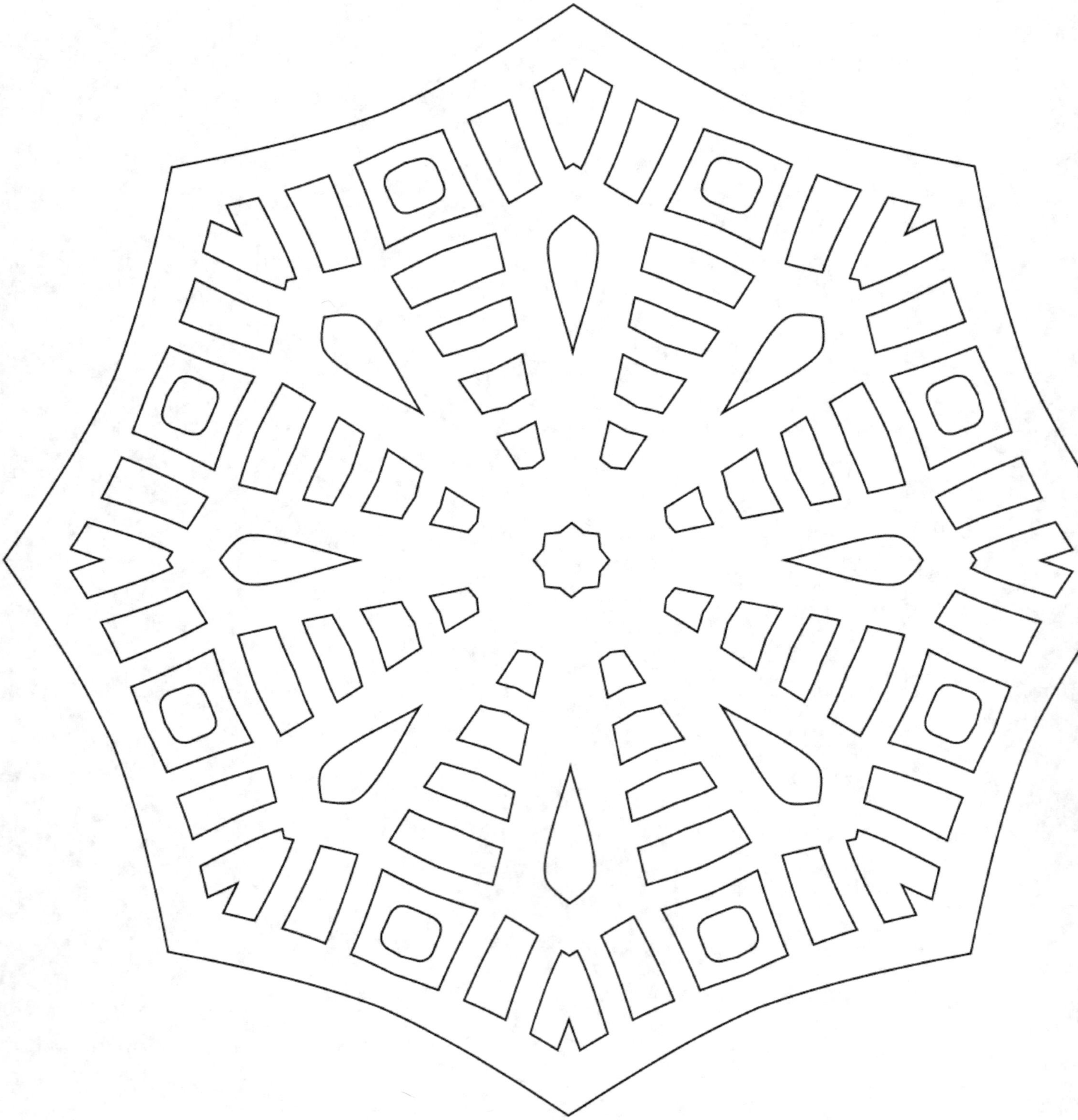

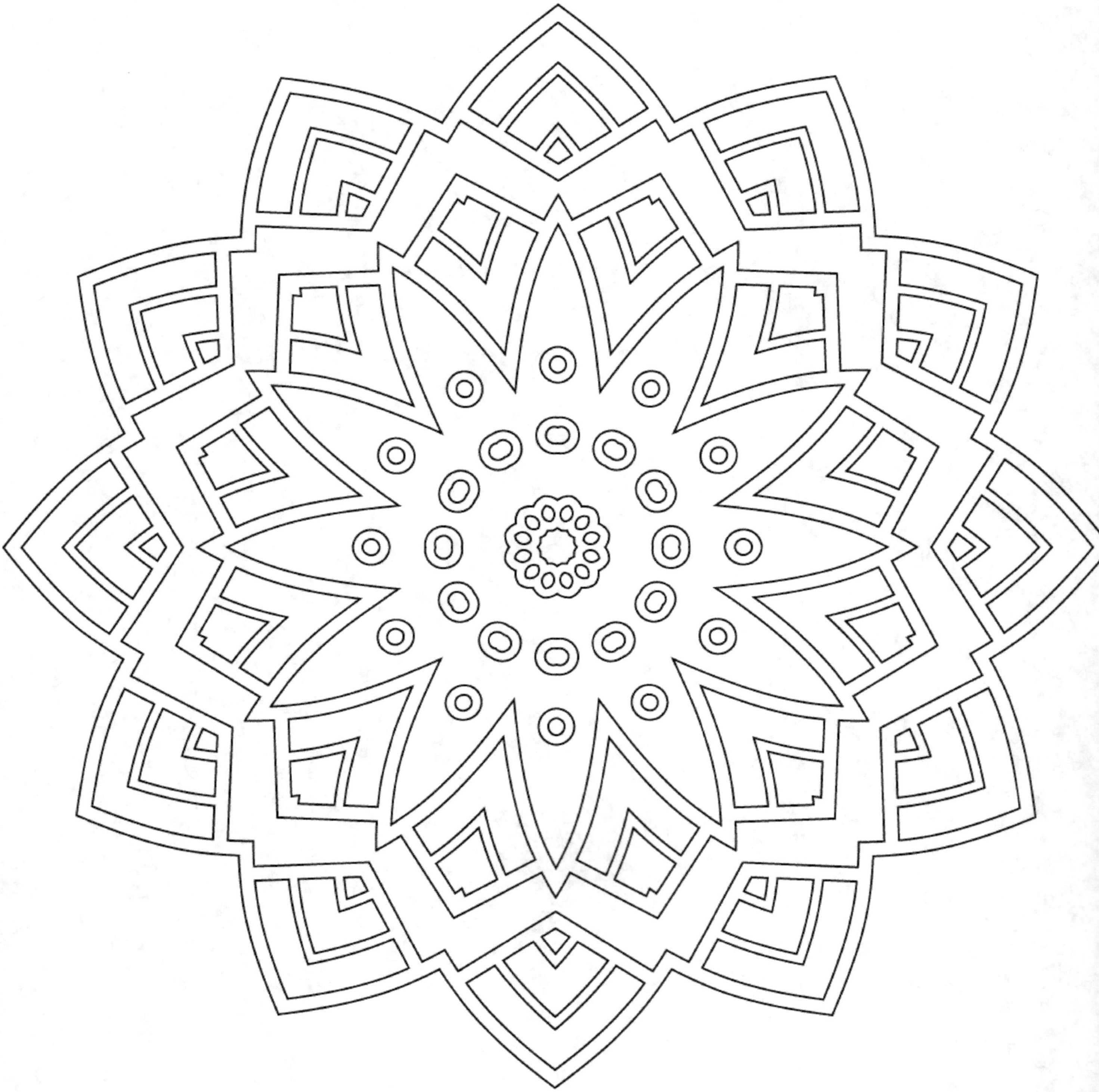

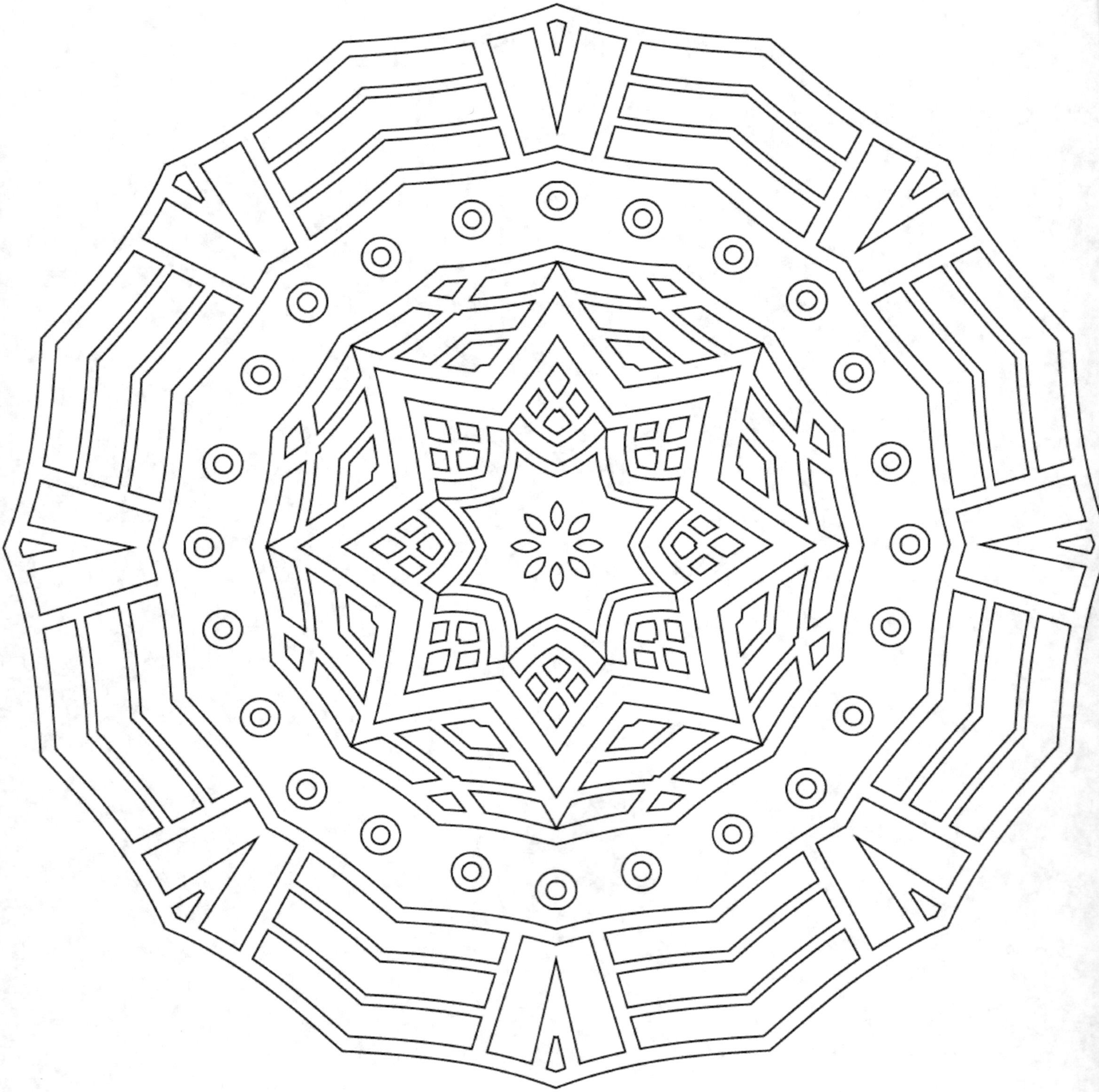

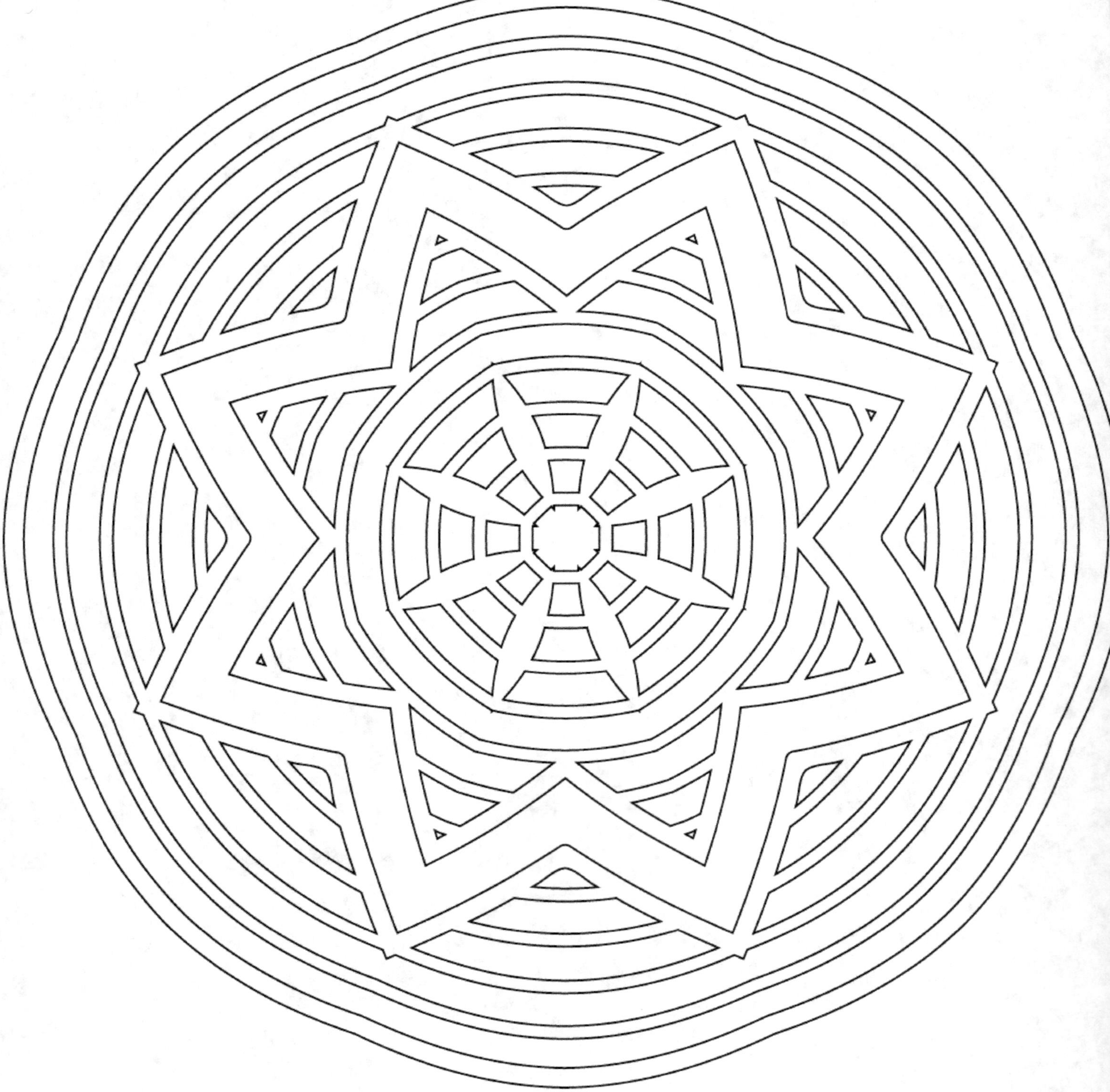

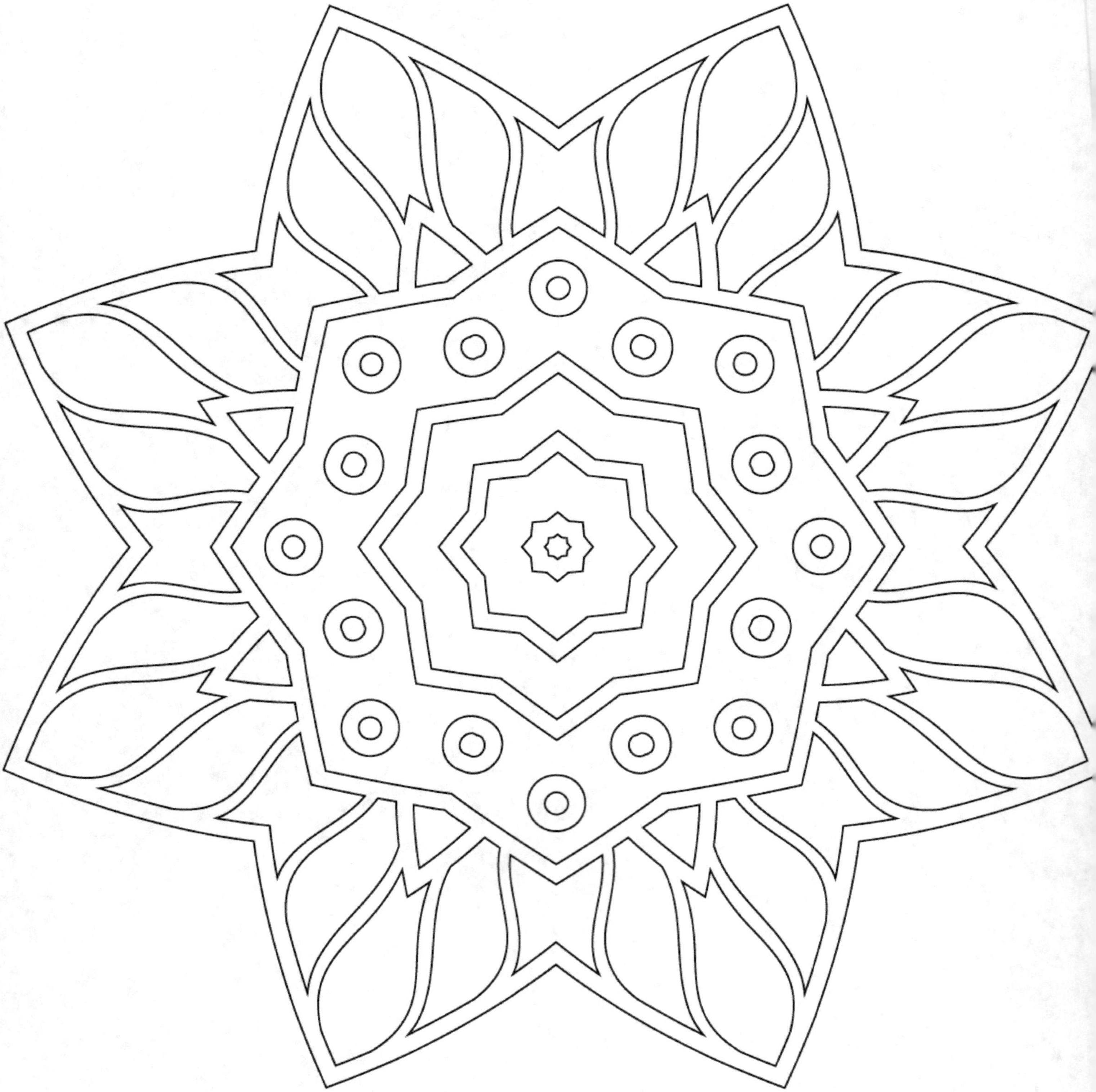

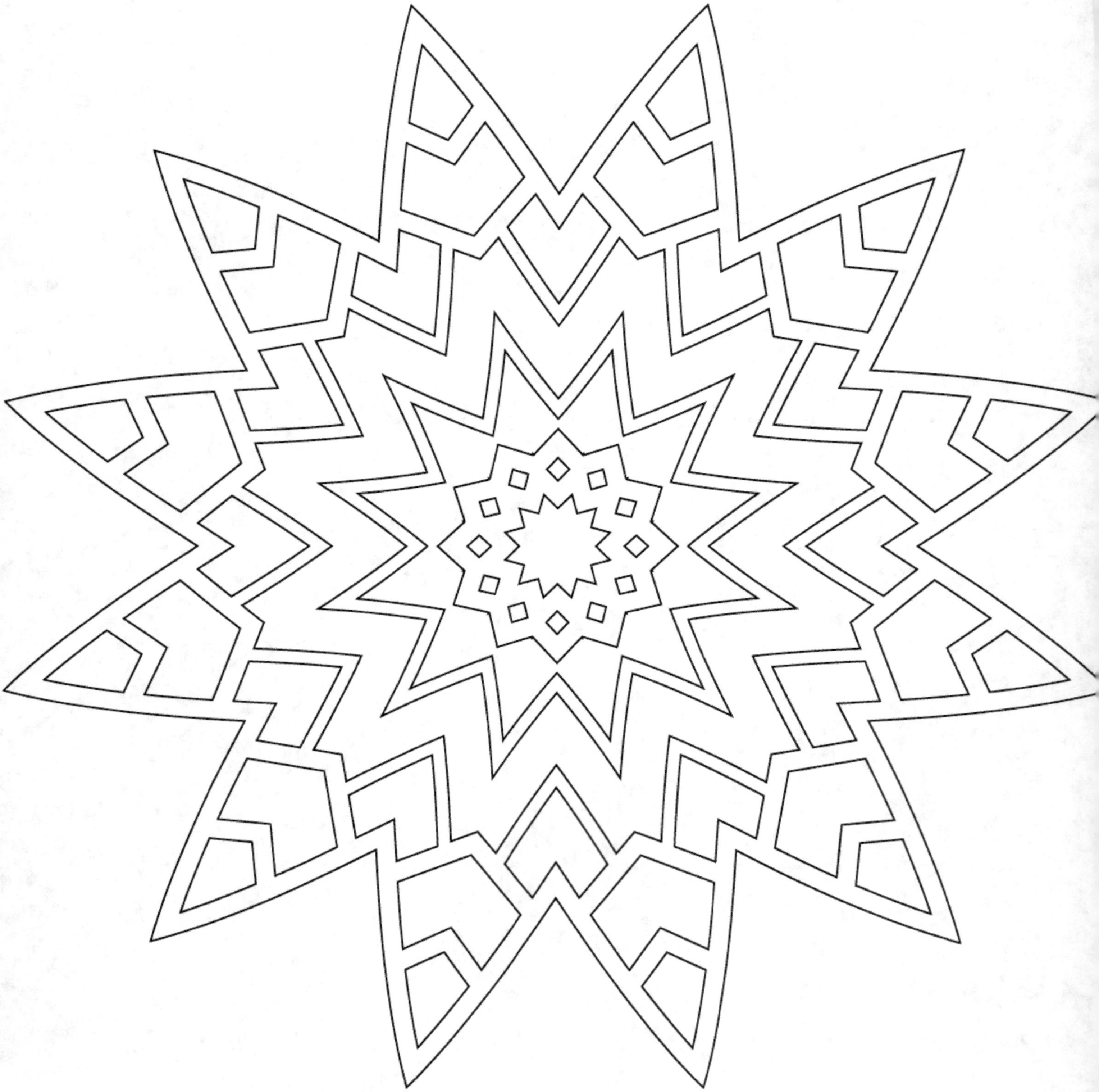

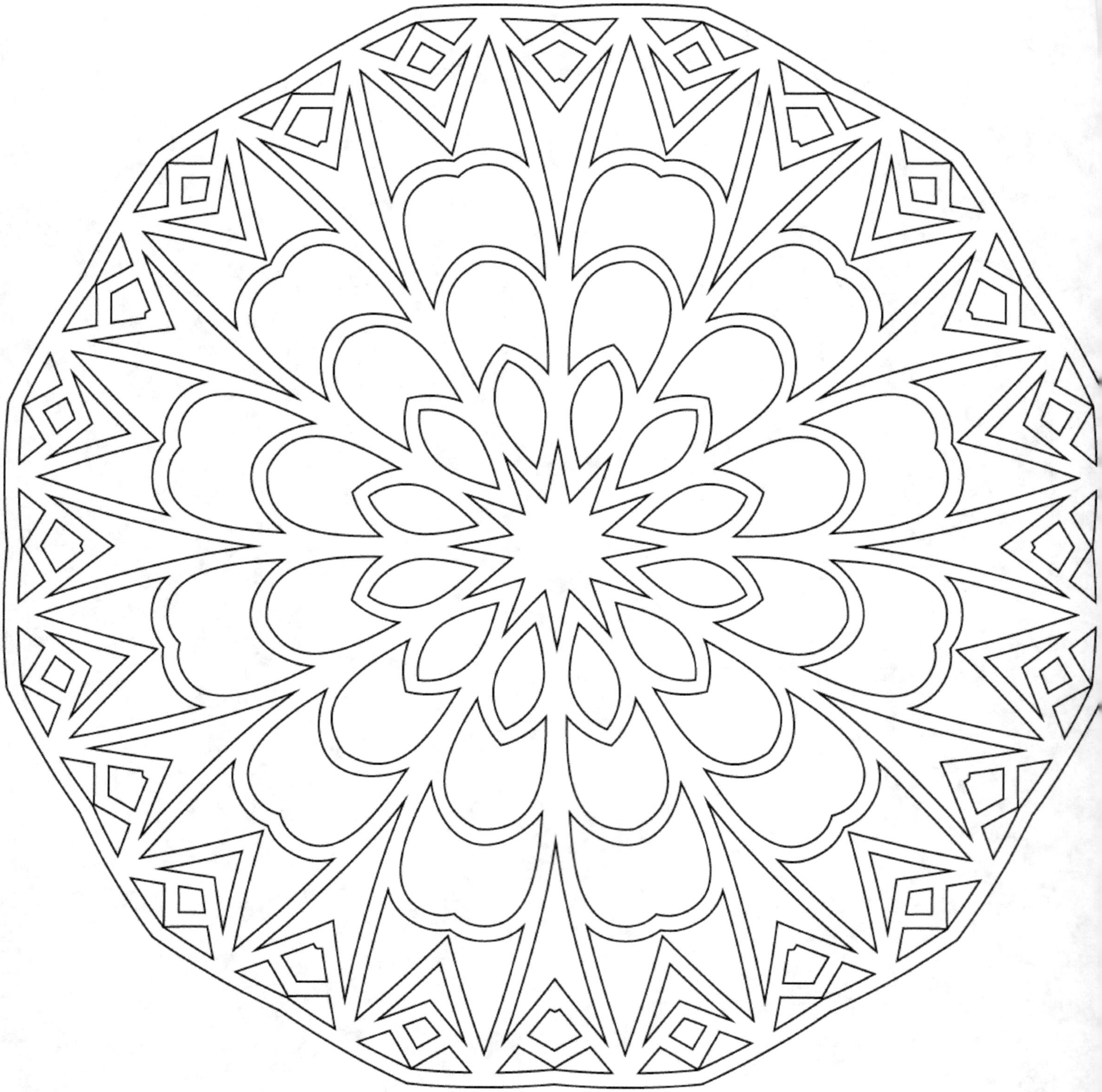

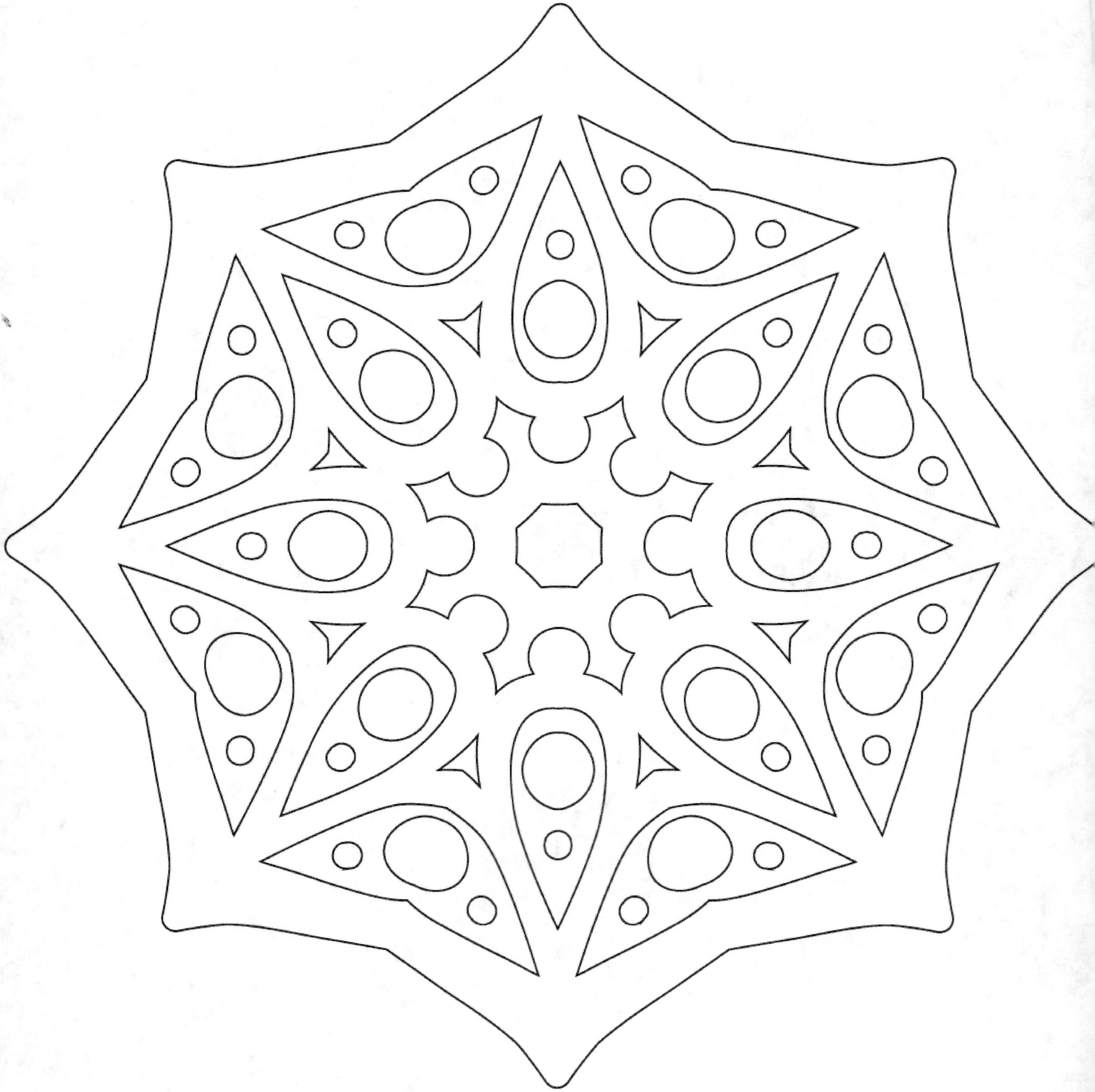

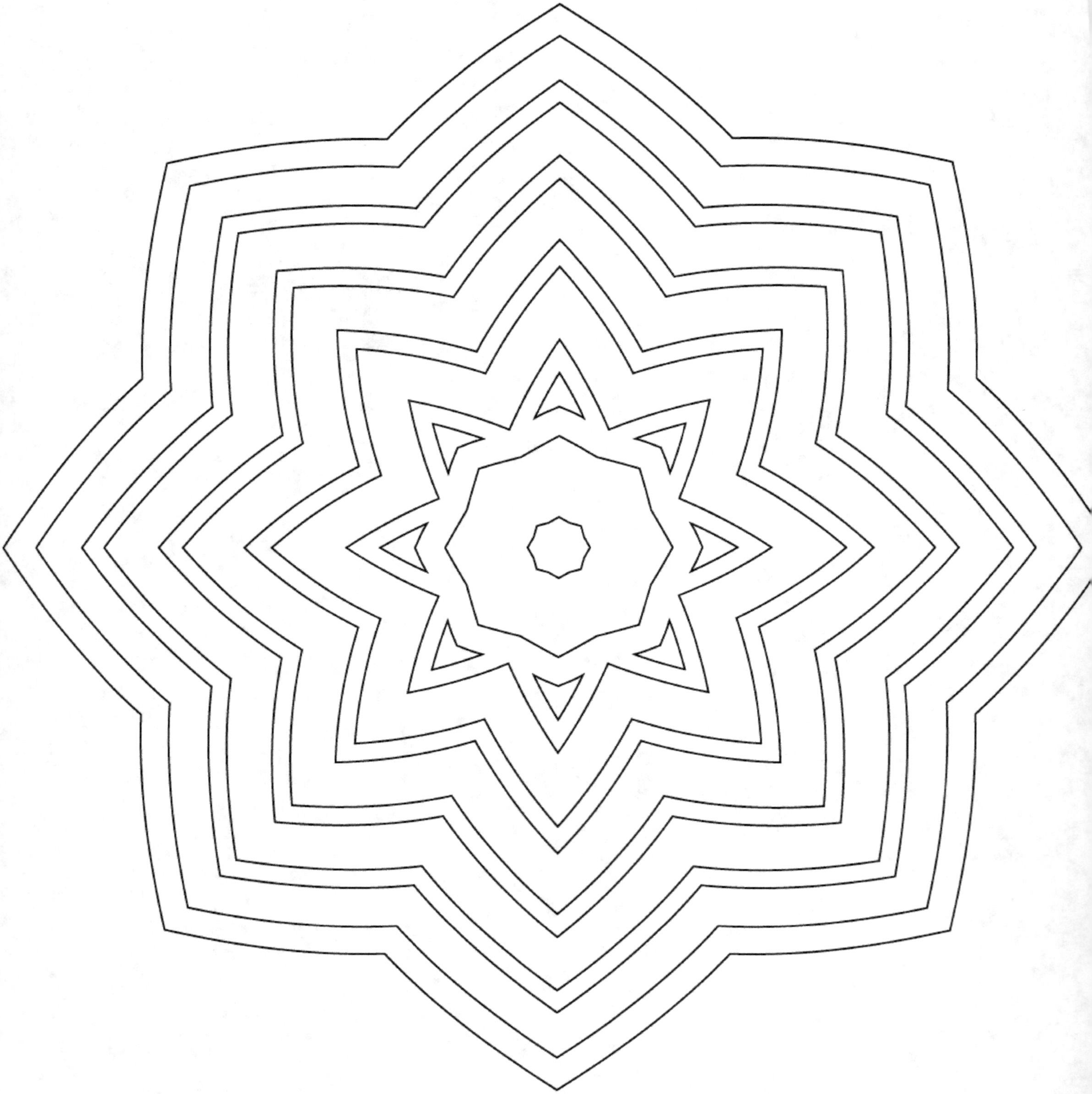

www.ingramcontent.com/pod-product-compliance
Lightning Source LLC
Chambersburg PA
CBHW080614220526
45466CB00010B/3346
* 9 7 9 8 5 6 3 9 6 8 7 7 6 *